creative

ARY SERVICES   IES

Thinking & Learning Skills

AGES 5-7

MIKE FLEETHAM
LYNNE WILLIAMS

D1137914

Authors
Mike Fleetham
Lynne Williams

Development Editor
Kate Pedlar

Editor
Caroline Carless

Project Editor
Fabia Lewis

Series Designers
Anthony Long and
Joy Monkhouse

Designer
Andrea Lewis

Illustrations
Andy Keylock / Beehive Illustration and
Gemma Hastilow / Beehive Illustration

The publishers would like to thank:
Jonathan Le Fevre for permission to use his idea for the
thinking board.
Rosie, Izzy and Lucy Broadhurst for their artwork.
Goldsmith Infant School, Portsmouth for permission to
use photographs taken at the school.

Authors' dedications:
I would like to dedicate this book to Charlie and Edward
Hale – two very creative chaps. (MF)

I would like to offer my special thanks to my family –
for always being there and for believing in me – and
Andrew Pearce, Critical Skills Programme Manager for
Wales, for sharing ideas, inspiration and encouragement.
This book is for every child I have ever worked with –
they allow me to make a difference. I would also like
to thank the children, parents and staff of Glanffrwd
Infants School, Ynysybwl, South Wales who so willingly
try out my ideas and give me something to smile about
everyday! (LW)

Published by Scholastic Ltd,
Villiers House,
Clarendon Avenue,
Leamington Spa,
Warwickshire CV32 5PR

www.scholastic.co.uk

Text © 2008 Mike Fleetham and Lynne Williams
© 2008 Scholastic Ltd

Designed using Adobe Indesign

Printed in China through Golden Cup Printing
Services.

1 2 3 4 5 6 7 8 9   8 9 0 1 2 3 4 5 6 7

British Library Cataloguing-in-
Publication Data

A catalogue record for this book is available from the
British Library.

ISBN 978-1407-10005-0

The rights of Mike Fleetham and Lynne Williams to be
identified as the authors of this work have been asserted
by them in accordance with the Copyright, Designs and
Patents Act 1988.

Contents

4 Introduction

Chapter One:

Get thinking: get learning!

8 Build a brain

10 Learner's backpack

12 Learner identity cards

14 Construct a team

16 Learning spies

18 World's biggest problem

20 Le Fevre teaching board

Chapter Two:

Thinking, learning and literacy

28 Magic printing machine

30 Build an author

32 Freddy's letter home

34 Journalists' den

36 Once upon a time

Chapter Three:

Thinking, learning, numeracy and science

44 Alien number abduction

46 Shape Land people

48 Celebrate with me

50 The number worm

52 Multi-coloured lab coat

Chapter Four:

Thinking, learning and the humanities

60 You're history

62 Time traveller

64 Pirate islands

Chapter Five:

Thinking, learning and the creative arts

70 Music box tales

72 Group paintbox

74 Under the sea

76 Monster pizza

78 Painting carousel

Chapter Six:

Thinking, learning and PE

86 All-team rounders

88 The jungle dance

90 Alien walk

92 On safari

Introduction

Why teach the skills of thinking and learning?

Success in life and learning now depends as much on having the right skills as it does on knowing the right things. Educational experts and business people such as Sir Ken Robinson, Professor Howard Gardner and Stan Shih, link a country's future success to its workforce's ability to think, learn and create. Therefore, our young children need opportunities to develop these skills from the moment they start school – not as an afterthought just before they begin work. The creative activities in this book provide an introduction to the skills that the 21st century will demand of them.

Categorising the skills of thinking and learning

There are many, many ways to categorise the skills of thinking and learning. The 29 activities in this book all use a straightforward model with eight main skills. These skills are not exclusive, but are illustrative of the important features of thinking and learning.

These eight main skills can be split into various sub-skills, such as:

● Managing thoughts: handling facts and ideas by sorting, sequencing, remembering, finding out, comparing and arranging.

● Creating thoughts: having new thoughts and ideas through synthesising, creating and innovating.

● Using thoughts: applying facts, thoughts and ideas by evaluating, problem solving, questioning, enquiring, critical thinking and making decisions.

● Thinking about thinking: reflecting on the management, creation and use of thoughts via the processes of metacognition, planning thinking, monitoring thinking and evaluating thinking.

● Collaboration: learning effectively with others through teamwork, cooperating, leading and organising.

● Independence: learning alone through self-motivation, taking risks, persevering, enterprise and handling change.

● Engagement: defining learning preferences and subject interest by looking at learning styles, learning readiness,

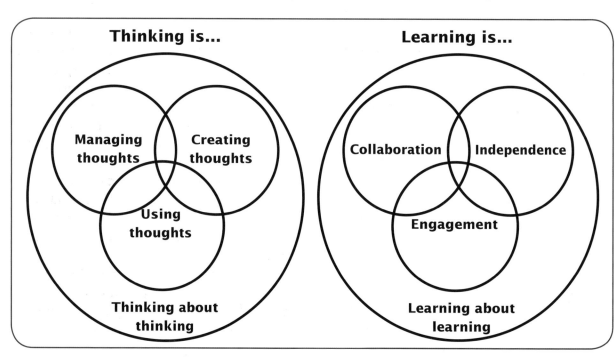

intelligence profiles, preferred subjects and dreams.

● Learning about learning: assessing learning through self-knowledge, reflecting on the learning process and target setting.

● The diagram on page 4 shows that the three central skills of 'Thinking' overlap each other and are surrounded by the fourth skill – 'Thinking about thinking'. The 'Learning' half of the diagram is organised in the same way to show how everything fits together. The boundaries between the skills and sub-skills are not always clear-cut so there will inevitably be some overlap between the two halves.

Variety of skills

Rather than targeting a single skill in each activity, this book provides opportunities for children to experience a variety of the sub-skills. After all, this is how the real world works: we are required to use multiple skills to achieve an end product. The full range of thinking and learning skills is covered across the 30 activities, thus regular inclusion of these creative activities in teaching sessions over a year will guarantee full skill coverage. Children will get many chances to develop each skill area and build up their experience at a pace which suits them. Share your successes with these activities at *www.thinkingclassroom.co.uk* and download extra ideas.

How to use this book

This book can be used on its own or with its companion (*Creative Activities: Thinking and Learning Skills 7–11*) to provide coverage right across the primary age and ability range. The skills introduced in this book are developed further through the activities in the 7–11 book. Younger learners who are ready can attempt the 7–11 activities while older children who need support may benefit from the 5–7 activities. As far as possible,

the contexts have been chosen to suit all ages from 5 to 11.

How to use the activities in this book

Each activity takes only one or two teaching sessions and combines a range of creative learning skills with important curriculum objectives, allowing you to develop your children's thinking and learning skills alongside curriculum subjects. The activities are described clearly and include instructions on how to set up and run the activity and evaluate the outcome at the end. They are divided into five curriculum-linked chapters (2–6) with Chapter 1 introducing thinking and learning skills. Consider using the first chapter before any of the others – these activities prepare children to develop their thinking and learning skills before tackling the curriculum-linked tasks. The introduction to each chapter provides some background information. Then each activity follows the same format: Setting the context, The challenge (problem), Objectives, You will need, Preparation, What to do (solving the problem), Drawing together, Support and Extension.

Objectives

These cover curriculum areas as well as thinking and learning skills. For example: a curriculum objective could be to know number bonds to 20. For the same task, the learning skill objective could be to work successfully in a group of three, while the thinking skill objective could be to compare and sort numbers by set criteria.

Preparation

This section includes anything that needs to be done before the lesson: this might include trying out an activity beforehand or making sample products for the children to look at during a task. In some activities there is an opportunity for role play as part of an imaginary scenario. Consider how you would do this, whether you might dress up yourself or invite another adult to take on this role.

What to do

This is a step-by-step explanation of how to carry out the activity and enable the children to solve the problem, often in an imaginary context introduced at the beginning of the lesson. It is your guide for delivering the activity and includes questions and directions for the class. Children may be required to work individually, in pairs or in groups.

Drawing together

Directions for the plenary session include information to support peer assessment and assessment for learning. Some activities include a 'Levels of success' assessment chart similar to the example below. As more activities are experienced, it is important to involve children in developing their own success grids: this can take place where 'Levels of success' charts are not provided. Before the children begin a main task, ask them what a fantastic result would look and sound like; what one that was nearly there would look and sound like and what one that needed more effort would look and sound like. Record their answers and refer to them during and after the task.

Differentiation

Ideas for supporting and extending children are given both in terms of the curriculum objectives or the thinking and learning skills required for each task.

Photocopiable pages

Many of the activities come with photocopiable resources. These can be found at the end of each chapter and may be photocopied for use in the classroom. More information on this book can be found at www.thinkingclassroom.co.uk.

Example of a 'Levels of success' chart

Not there yet ☆	Nearly there ☆ ☆	Fantastic ☆ ☆ ☆
✔ Kept the sentences muddled ✔ Worked alone	✔ Un-muddled 1 short sentence ✔ Thought up a new use for the machine ✔ Worked in a pair	✔ Un-muddled 2 long sentences ✔ Thought up a really imaginative use for the machine ✔ Worked really well in a pair and a four

Chapter One

Get thinking: get learning!

- Build a brain   8
- Learner's backpack   10
- Learner identity cards   12
- Construct a team   14
- Learning spies   16
- World's biggest problem   18
- Le Fevre teaching board   20

The activities in this chapter teach children the key skills for improving their thinking and learning. It is advisable to start with this chapter because it covers the fundamental skills which children can then apply to subject specific tasks in the rest of the book.

We begin with **Build a brain** in which children design a brain for a robot of a particular size within strict time parameters.

Learner's backpack requires children to create a set of learning tools. A learner's backpack, like a builder's tool box, contains everything needed to do a job properly. But learners need more than equipment: they also need less concrete things such as learning strategies and personal qualities.

In **Learner identity cards**, children are asked to consider the qualities needed to learn effectively. This knowledge can boost learning esteem and help children to understand and work with others.

Construct a team encourages children to value the skills of their peers and explores how a strong team can be built. Collaborative activities such as this create situations where pupils can share ideas, pool their resources and teach and assess each other – all features of effective learning.

Learning spies enables children to differentiate between learning something and simply 'doing the work'. They explore learning in practice and look for evidence of learning around the school. By finding out what learning looks, sounds and feels like, they will get a better idea of what they're aiming for during lessons.

In **World's biggest problem**, the problem itself is to find the largest problem in the world. This requires you to develop, with your children, criteria for spotting a problem and comparing the size of problems.

Finally, **Le Fevre teaching board** gives guidance on how you, as a teacher, can monitor thinking and learning progress throughout the school year, using Jonathan Le Fevre's method of mind-mapping.

Build a brain

Setting the context
Dr Neuron is a famous brain scientist and you are her assistant. You are helping her to build a robot to lend a hand with experiments. She has almost finished! The only thing left to make is the brain. When that's done you can pop it inside the robot's metal head and switch it on. Building a robot brain is a tricky job but with the right tools, materials and some help from you, Dr Neuron is bound to succeed.

The challenge
Dr Neuron is away at a conference but she has told you what the brain needs to do and has left everything you will need. Can you finish the brain before she returns?

Objectives
To develop creative and independent working skills within strict time limits and with limited resources.
To know that the brain is used for thinking and for controlling the body.
To know that the brain has different parts which do different things.

You will need
Copies of photocopiable page 22; colouring pens; sheets of A5 card; safe access to pairs of scissors; a limited, clearly defined selection of objects, for example: three lollipop sticks, three coloured balls of Plasticine®, three sequins or buttons, three coloured pipe cleaners. You will also need a visible way to count down 20 minutes such as a classroom clock or a sand timer and a small shoebox for limiting and checking the size of each child's robot brain.

Preparation
If you dress up as Dr Neuron for the plenary you will need to prepare your costume, for example, a white lab coat and stethoscope. Materials for the children can be gathered together and placed in plastic dishes before the lesson begins. Copy the 'Levels of success' chart, onto a whiteboard or a flipchart to refer to with the children.

What to do
● Read the context and problem to the children.
● Show them an enlarged version of the photocopiable on page 22.
● Let the children ask questions about the plan.
● Point out the requirements and success criteria for the task:
  1. You must use all of your resources – nothing can be left over.
  2. Your brain must have four labelled parts: one for thoughts, one for making words, one for moving the body and one for storing pictures.

Photograph © 2008, JupiterImages Corporation

Illustration © 2008, Andy Keylock / Beehive Illustration

3. Your brain can have one extra part that you invent.

4. Your brain must fit inside a small shoebox (this is the same size as the robot's head).

5. You must build the brain on your own and finish it within 20 minutes.

● Ask the children to tell a partner what Dr Neuron has asked them to do.

● Give them an opportunity to clarify their understanding with you.

● Explain that they will have only 20 minutes to build the brain before Dr Neuron returns.

● Tell them that they will be working independently.

Illustration © 2008, Andy Keylock / Beehive Illustration

Drawing together

● Dress up as Dr Neuron and play the role of a brain scientist.

● Ask the children to look at their finished brains and assess how well they have met the criteria that were set.

● Demonstrate how to assess the task using the chart below, then allow the children to assess each other's brains (a brain may meet criteria from different columns, but each brain should, ideally, fulfil all the criteria of one column before moving up to the next level).

● Encourage children to ask questions about each other's brains.

Support

● Allow less dextrous learners to work in pairs.

● The task could be made easier by limiting resources, extending time limits or through adapting the success criteria.

Extension

Encourage children to find out more information about the brain and make suggestions for modifications to their models.

Page
9

Levels of success

Not there yet ☆	Nearly there ☆ ☆	Fantastic ☆ ☆ ☆
✔ Some materials used	✔ Most materials used	✔ All materials used
✔ Worked alone	✔ 3 correctly labelled parts	✔ 4 correctly labelled parts
✔ 2 or fewer labelled parts	✔ Finished after 20 minutes	✔ 1 extra labelled part
✔ Not finished yet		✔ Fits in a small shoebox
✔ Bigger than small shoebox		✔ Finished within 20 minutes

Learner's backpack

Illustration © 2008, Andy Keylock / Beehive Illustration

Setting the context

Dr Marco, the wise old man of Cognitam, has just built a new school. It's not like other schools because it is magically hidden down a secret passage between two large buildings. The buildings are so big and shiny that no one notices the tiny alleyway sandwiched there. If you squeeze along this passage you will find Dr Marco's new school. It's fab! Everyone gets to learn what they want to, when they want to – and in a way that suits them! Dr Marco has invited you to spend a week there but he wants you to pack your bag first. And he wants a little more than usual. He knows that you'll bring a pencil and a ruler, but he also wants to know what skills and qualities you'll be bringing – skills like 'listening' and 'turn-taking' and qualities such as 'helping others' and 'being a hard worker'.

The challenge

Can you find 50 items to put in your backpack to take to Cognitam?

Objectives

To know at least three different pieces of learning equipment, three different learning skills and three learning qualities.
To know that learning needs equipment, resources, skills and personal qualities.
To develop collaboration and teamwork skills.

You will need

Copies of photocopiable page 23 for each group (enlarged to A3 size if required); pencils; some glue or Blu-Tack® for fixing labels onto the backpacks; safe access to pairs of scissors.

Preparation

Set up a classroom wall display showing a large, empty backpack. The title could be 'Our learning backpack' or 'What do we need to learn well?'. Photocopy page 23 for each group – enlarging it and printing it onto A3 paper if preferred. Before you begin the activity, copy the 'Levels of success' chart onto a whiteboard or a flipchart to refer to with the children.

What to do

● Share the scenario about Dr Marco's new school with the children and let them ask questions for clarification.
● Discuss what learning equipment, skills and qualities are (anything that helps us to build up our learning) and give examples: *a pencil because you can write down facts and draw diagrams; a book because you can find out information; a computer because you can communicate with other learners; asking questions because that's how to get people to teach you; choosing because that's how you decide what to learn and how to learn it, listening because that's one way to find out things; being organised because that's how you make sure you get everything done; being confident because that helps you not to give up.*
● Show the children the display that you have started and explain that you need everyone's help to complete it. Explain that the display will be up all year and more labels and photographs will be added.

- Arrange the children into groups of two or three (depending on the current level of their group work) and allocate the following jobs:

    1. Leader – he or she makes sure everyone has a say and that the job gets done.

    2. Writer – this person's job is to write, inside the blanks on page 23 (before they are cut out) and stick them onto the backpack.

    3. Talker – he or she cuts out the blanks on page 23 and speaks on behalf of the group. In a group of two, the leader can also be the talker.

- Tell the children to discuss their ideas in their groups. When they have agreed on a skill, they should add it to their copies of photocopiable page 23, next to the appropriate symbol each time (hand, hammer or face).

- Share the success criteria: 'Your group must make a learning backpack with at least six things inside: two must be equipment (the hammers); two must be skills (the hands); two must be qualities (the faces). Each person must do their own job in the group. The backpack must be finished within 20 minutes.'

Drawing together

- Ask the talker from each group to share one thing from their backpack with the rest of the class, explaining what it is and why it has been included in the backpack. As each group does this, add their examples to the large class backpack.

- Ask each group to assess their backpack using the success criteria in the chart below.

Support

- Help children may find the activity difficult by providing worksheets with part-completed equipment/skills/qualities for them to fill in.

- Use images and symbols, for example, '?' for asking questions and two-headed arrows for making choices.

- Extend the time limit or restrict the concepts to concrete examples of equipment and introduce the skills and qualities later on.

Extension

Take photos of learning equipment, skills and qualities being used well and stick them next to the appropriate symbol. Select pieces of work that illustrate the good use of equipment/skills/qualities (for example, straight lines with a ruler or interesting questions) and add these to the display.

Photograph © 2008, JupiterImages Corporation

Levels of success

Not there yet ☆	Nearly there ☆☆	Fantastic ☆☆☆
✔ Between 0 and 5 things in the backpack	✔ 6 things in backpack	✔ More than 6 things in backpack
✔ People swapped jobs or didn't do them	✔ Skills/ qualities – less than 2	✔ Skills/ qualities/ equipment – 2 or more
✔ Not finished yet	✔ People did their jobs	✔ Everyone did their job well
	✔ Finished after 20 minutes	✔ Finished within 20 minutes

Learner identity cards

Setting the context

The Government has decided that every pupil must have a learner identity card. The cards will show how each pupil prefers to learn as well as the things that they do best. The card must be carried at all times when in school and shown to a teacher if they ask to see it. The Government hopes that learner identity cards will improve learning right across the country because pupils and teachers will know more about learning.

The challenge

Government inspectors will be making a surprise visit to all schools this week so you will need to have your identity cards at the ready!

Objectives

To know at least three individual learning preferences.
To understand the value of thinking about learning.
To explore and evaluate learning preferences.

You will need

One blank identity card and a pencil for each learner (you could photocopy the top half of photocopiable page 24 onto thick card and cut out enough to give one to each child); copies of photocopiable page 24 (bottom half) for each pair.

Preparation

If the 'inspectors' are going to visit the class then arrange for colleagues or visitors to play these roles. You will find that having a real audience will sharpen the children's focus! Ask the 'inspectors' to complete an ID card themselves so that they will be able to give genuine feedback to the children.

What to do

● Ask the children to think about a recent lesson, maybe the last one, and discuss their views: what did they learn? What did they do while they were learning? They should think about whether everyone did the same thing and if everyone enjoyed the lesson the same amount. Ask them to think about whether children learn in different ways to each other and what different ways there are to learn.

● Tell them about you as a learner. Include your preferences relating to seeing, hearing,

Illustration © 2008, Andy Keylock / Beehive Illustration

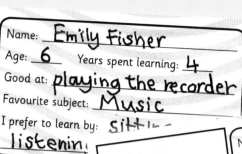

Name: Emily Fisher
Age: 6 **Years spent learning:** 4
Good at: playing the recorder
Favourite subject: Music
I prefer to learn by: sittin-
listenin_

Valid from: Sept_

Name: aaron Carter
Age: 7 **Years spent learning:** 7
Good at: science
Favourite subject: swimming, reading
I prefer to learn by: talking with others

Valid from: September 2008

MY LEARNER CARD

touching or moving. Do you prefer to work with other people or on your own? Do you prefer to work with music playing in the background or in silence?

● Explain your preferences for temperature and lighting and any other features you can think of.

● Describe a friend or colleague who learns in a different way to you.

● Ask the children to talk with a partner about how they prefer to learn, using the continuums on photocopiable page 24 as a starting point for their discussions. Regroup as a whole class and discuss the outcomes.

● Talk the children through filling in the blank identity cards. You may wish to dedicate several short sessions to this.

● Draw up some assessment criteria as a class to refer to when the activity has been completed.

Drawing together

● When the ID cards have been made, invite the 'inspectors' into the classroom. Ask the children to take it in turns to present their ID cards to the inspectors and encourage the children to ask the inspectors questions and vice versa.

● Ask the children to work in pairs and consider how they would make a good team if their learning styles are different. Ask them to compare cards and see if preferring one way of learning helps them to enjoy a particular subject more than another.

● Finish the session by asking the children to evaluate their ID cards against the criteria they decided on as a class.

● Plan to use the cards in the future maybe as a display or refer to them during future lessons.

Support

● Allow children to take a blank ID card home to discuss it with their parents/carers first, to give them some ideas as a starting point. Less confident learners could focus on a few of the items on the ID card and give concrete examples.

● To help generate ideas, allow children to talk about their choices with you or a friend (watch out for children 'copying' each other's preferences.)

Extension

● It is important that the children know that the learning profile shown on their ID card is not fixed. Tell them that it can change over time and that you will review the cards later in the term.

● Ask the children to add additional preferences that are not shown and invite them to compare and contrast their ID card with another child's.

Construct a team

Setting the context
If we work together, it can be easier to get a job done. Everyone's good at something different. Someone might be a good writer or a good talker; someone else might be better at drawing or building or leading other children. If we put all these people in a group, then they can do a lot more than someone working on their own.

The challenge
Work as a team – where every member has a particular role – to make a small poster about yourselves within 30 minutes.

Objectives
To develop teamwork skills and to be able to contribute to a shared task.
To reflect on one's own learning within a group.

You will need
A set of team role cards from the photocopiable page 25; some flipchart paper and an easel for each group.

Preparation
This activity will tell you where your children are with team-working and what you need to work on to develop their skills. You may wish to put everyone randomly in groups of three or four to see what happens or you may wish to think about the groupings beforehand. Some children may still not be ready to work with others, some may be comfortable in pairs and others may even be ready for larger groups – fours or fives.

While we do not want to set them up to fail, a perfect collaboration gives you less feedback for improvement than one that doesn't quite work. Try to put the children in a situation just a tiny bit beyond their skill level and a toe or two outside their comfort zone.

What to do
● Arrange the children into groups and explain to them that you want to find out about their team-work skills.
● Explain the task in more detail: within their team they need to give everyone a special job in order to create a poster. The poster should include: a name for their team, a picture of each person and each person's name. The poster must be completed within 30 minutes and then presented to the rest of the class.
● Ask the children within each team to choose who does what and talk them through the role cards (taken from the photocopiable on page 25).
● As a class, create a set of success criteria to refer to at the end of the activity.
● Let the children begin and step back to observe and record what you see and hear. Write down positive, negative and interesting things that you see and hear, ready to share with the children.

Photograph © 2008, JupiterImages Corporation

● Focus on how the children fulfil each of their roles and how effectively they work together as a team. It might be quite chaotic: this is not failure, but a step towards teaching them the skills they need.

Drawing together
● Ask each group to present their poster and continue to record what you see and hear.
● Then, ask the children to think about the original task and the role cards and to think about how well they think they did. Refer back to the success criteria you created at the start of the activity.
● Share some of your observations but withhold judgement for now. For example: '*I heard Jemma asking Billy what he thought.*', '*I saw Kyle grab the pen from his team's writer!*', '*I heard Suzie say that you have to take turns.*
● Ask the children to share one thing that went really well in their group and record their answers on one half of a flipchart page. Ask them to think of one thing they would like to change next time they work in a team and record these on the other half of the page. If the children miss something important, add this yourself (for example, 'We need to listen to each other').

● Stick the page onto a display board in the classroom and refer to it from now on – tick the things that went well as they are repeated in further teamwork, and tick the problems as they are solved.

Support
● Divide the children into smaller groups or pairs, consisting of a talker and a writer, if the children cannot cope with larger groups.
● Allow more time to make the task easier. You could also choose to display the children's posters instead of asking the children to present them.

Extension
You can challenge the children by developing team roles and making them specific to a particular task. For example, if artwork is needed, create an Artist role. Extend the activity by editing the role cards to include more detailed task descriptions. Alternatively, ask the children to change roles so that they are developing a range of skills and organise them into different groups.

Learning spies

Setting the context

Rumour has it that some learning has been taking place in school. The headteacher is very interested and wants to find out more. However, it can be very difficult to track down learning and then catch it – especially when it's actually taking place. You usually only see it when it's over! It's a bit like solving a crime. A situation like this calls for the specialist learning spies. These people are an elite bunch who understand learning and how to find it. They are highly skilled at following the clues to learning and then catching it before it can run away. They are people just like you!

The challenge

Can you find at least three different things about learning around the classroom or school and then report your findings to the headteacher?

Objectives

To be able to describe at least three features of learning.
To know what learning looks like, sounds like and feels like.
To become more confident at risk-taking, cooperating and independent learning.

You will need

A magnifying glass, digital camera and audio recorder (alternatively just use copies of photocopiable page 26); a pencil or pen and a clipboard and copies of photocopiable page 26 for each learning detective/group.

Preparation

Choose a 'Learning Spies Week' in which all children get the chance to be learning spies. They will be sent off around the school building and grounds to find out where learning is taking place. Plan for them to go off, with adult support, for a set time (30 minutes to an hour) in pairs or threes during the week. Warn your colleagues, support staff, office staff and others working in the school that this will be happening and prepare them for

Image © 2008 JupiterImages Corporation

the children's questions and investigations. Prepare a checklist of learning clues to use at the start of the activity.

What to do

● Read out the problem to the children and ask them what they might be looking for. Make a checklist which should include what you hear when learning is happening; what you see when

learning is happening; what people might be feeling when they are learning; what people do when they are learning.
● Guide the children as much as is necessary, possibly by modelling for them several key features of learning through a variety of examples, such as: someone asking or answering a question, a TV programme/DVD/video being watched, two people having a discussion, someone saying their spellings/times tables, a teacher reading a book, the site manager making a phone call to a plumber, the school secretary writing an email message.
● Ask them to record on a copy of the worksheet from photocopiable page 26, what they are aiming to find.
● During the week, send the children off around the school in small groups.

Drawing together

● At the end of the week, organise a session when the children can regroup as a class to report their findings to each other.
● Invite the headteacher to come and listen to what the children have seen and heard and to ask them questions.
● Record and display the evidence then challenge the children to recreate the same behaviours in their own learning.

Support

● Group less confident learners with others who can support them. Provide examples of evidence that is easy to discover (for example, someone finding something out from a book or the internet) as well as images of what the children are seeking (for example a photo of someone using a computer).
● Alter the time spent out of class 'detecting' to allow children to have more time if they need it.

Extension

● Allow the children to interview pupils who they believe are learning, by asking questions such as: *Are you learning? What are you learning? How do you know you are learning?*
● Provide cameras so that the children can take photos of learning taking place and create a display of all the evidence collected. With appropriate adult supervision or set as a homework task, the children could seek evidence of learning outside of school.

World's biggest problem

Photograph © 2008, JupiterImages Corporation

Setting the context

There was a story in the paper yesterday about a bus that was too tall to fit under a bridge. The grown-ups couldn't agree what to do. 'Make the bridge higher!' some said. 'Too expensive,' others replied. 'Cut a bit off the top of the bus!' they insisted. 'Too difficult,' said the first lot. Then a little boy called Louis piped up, 'Let down the tyres. It'll fit through then.' And it did! The grown-ups were so impressed that they made Louis their king and chief problem-solver. They came to him from dawn to dusk with their challenges. He solved every single one and eventually became very bored. No one could really stretch his abilities. So he decided to ask the children of the land if they could help him. 'Find me the biggest problem in the world!' he shouted. And off they went to do just that...

The challenge

Can you find the biggest problem in the world?

Objectives

To develop skills of reasoning and thinking across a number of subject areas.
To recognise a problem and begin to believe that every problem has a solution.
To know different definitions of 'problem'.
To learn how to evaluate and compare problems.

You will need

A whiteboard or flipchart; a plastic or card crown.

Preparation

Develop for yourself a working definition of 'problem' and a method for comparing 'size' (difficulty) of different problems. For example: a problem is a situation that stops someone doing what they want; a problem is a question that takes time to answer; a problem is when things do not go to plan; if it's solved and things get better, then it must have been a problem. When comparing and evaluating problems, consider for example, how many people are affected and how seriously. Think about how many people it takes to solve the problem and how long this takes. You will also need to consider if the problem has ever been solved. Have to mind a number of problems ranging from simple and close to home (such as children not lining up properly) to difficult and global (such as war). You may wish to draw up a list of guidelines for when the children are presenting to King Louis, or you may prefer to do this as a class activity during the task.

What to do

● Tell the children about a few real problems – include one that you've personally experienced, one from school and one from the news. Then ask the children to silently think of a problem that they have experienced or know about and to tell this problem to a partner. Between them they should come up with one or more solutions.
● Ask pairs to get together and share their six problems (three from each pair) and come

up with two more.

● Listen to one or two problems from the class, then ask the children to define what a problem is. Record their answers on a whiteboard or flipchart, and include your own examples in the discussion (see Preparation). As a class decide on a working definition of 'problem'.

● Take a brain break.

● Bring the children back together and ask pairs (or fours) to decide which of their problems is the biggest. Challenge them to explain how they decided which problem was the biggest and record their responses on a whiteboard or flipchart.

● Share the context and problem outlined above and challenge pairs (or fours) to prepare for an audience with King Louis at which they will present what they believe to be the world's biggest problem. Give the children some guidelines on how to present to King Louis, for example: bow as you approach the king, wait to be asked to speak, speak for no longer than one minute, speak loudly and clearly, tell the king your choice for the world's biggest problem and your reasons for choosing this problem, bow as you leave the king, never turn your back on the king. Display these guidelines on a whiteboard or flipchart for the children to refer to throughout the lesson.

Drawing together

● Put on your crown and, in turn, ask the children to come before you with their choice for 'The biggest problem in the world'. They must follow the presentation guidelines that you have displayed.

● Ask the audience to use the rules to assess a presenting pair (or four).

● Act out the role of King Louis and, as you give the children feedback, refer to the working definition of 'problem' and the children's ideas about deciding what makes a problem big.

● Post all of the children's chosen problems on a display board in the classroom and tell them you will think about which one is the biggest and get back to them!

Support

● Group less confident learners with those who can support their thinking about problems and their expression of them.

● Make the task easier by suggesting a range of problems for the children to consider and allowing them to decide which is the biggest.

● Alternatively, limit the problem choice to those with which the children have direct experience or restrict the problem to a particular subject area, such as, maths.

Extension

● Restrict the problems to those with which the children do not have direct experience, such as, world problems.

● Ask children to rank six problems in order, according to ease of solutions.

● After the initial task refine both the class definition of 'problem' and the criteria for evaluating difficulty.

Le Fevre teaching board

(a creative activity for teachers!)

Setting the context

We recommend that you include one of these creative activities each week. Over the teaching year, your children will get opportunities to develop a wide range of thinking and learning skills while simultaneously learning curriculum content. A Le Fevre teaching board is an excellent way to publicly value the skills that are being developed and to keep you and the children focused on these as well as the subjects. The idea was invented by Jonathan Le Fevre, a headteacher working in Hampshire.

The challenge

How can we easily and publicly value the thinking and learning skills that are being developed through these creative activities?

Objectives

To produce an interactive teaching board that clearly shows the full range of thinking and learning skills.
To consider how the board can evolve during a school year.
To involve the children in the use and development of the board.

You will need

A small display space near to the lesson delivery area; access to clipart/images; display-making materials and equipment; Velcro®.

Preparation

On a display near to your lesson delivery area, create a mind-map style display which includes: a central image to represent thinking and learning skills and which includes the phrase, 'How we think and learn' with six branches coming from the central image, each with a suitable image:

Illustration © 2008, Andy Keylock / Beehive Illustration

1. 'Having new thoughts'
2. 'Using my thoughts'
3. 'Knowing facts'
4. 'Working with others'
5. 'Working on my own'
6. 'Knowing how I learn'
Make sure that there is a piece of Velcro® by the image for each branch. Make six gold card stars and fix the opposite Velcro® on the back of each.

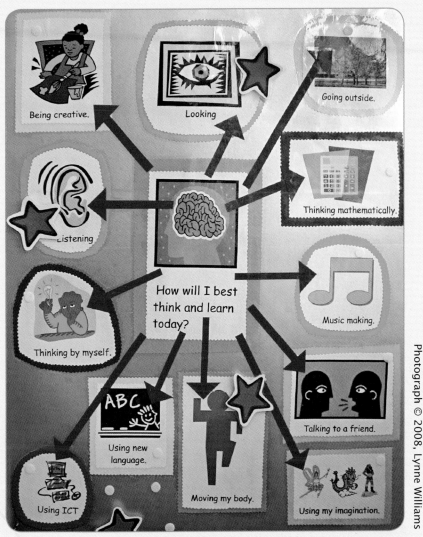

Photograph © 2008, Lynne Williams

What to do

● Your Le Fevre board is multi-purpose and can be adapted to different teaching and learning styles. Here are several ways to use it:

● At the beginning of a creative (or other) learning activity, tell the children which skills they will be developing and fix a star by each one.

● At the end of an activity, ask the children which skills they used and stick stars in the appropriate places.

● Make laminated name tags for each child and invite them to Blu-Tack® their name next to their best skill.

● Ask the children to nominate each other for using a skill well.

● As the skills are used more and more, add sub-branches, for example: using my thoughts – solving problems; answering questions; choosing.

● Add photos taken by the children and the children's work samples to the branches to show what the skills look like in practice.

● Make the display into a learning mat and give each child a laminated copy – they can then use a dry-wipe marker pen to assess their performance.

Drawing together

● Use the board in different ways and ask the children if they have any more ideas of how to use it. Allow them to suggest additions and improvements.

Support

● Use images and simple text to make the Le Fevre board more child-friendly.

● Reinforce the range of thinking and learning skills by giving the children several concrete examples of what a skill is and what it looks like.

Extension

● Extend the purpose of the board by adding metacognition branches such as 'Creativity looks like this'; 'Moving my body looks like this' and add further branches as new skills are addressed.

● You could even create a web-based board including video and audio clips, images, sounds, documents and animations.

Dr Neuron's plan for a robot brain

My robot brain needs to:

- make the robot's body move
- think
- make words for the robot's voice
- store what the robot's eyes see
- fit inside the robot's head

Labels:

| Thoughts here | Words made here | Body controlled here | Pictures stored here | |

Ideas and questions:

How can I fit all 4 parts into one small brain?

Should I join some parts together?

Which objects will be best for each part of the brain?

What extra part shall I add to the brain?

Our learning backpack

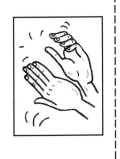 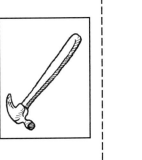 

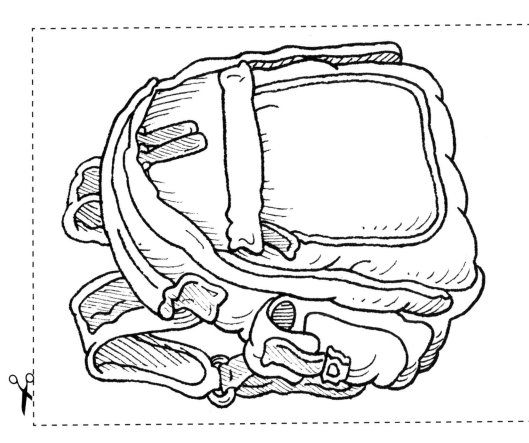

■SCHOLASTIC
www.scholastic.co.uk

PHOTOCOPIABLE   *Creative Activities for Thinking and Learning Skills: Ages 5-7*

Learner ID card

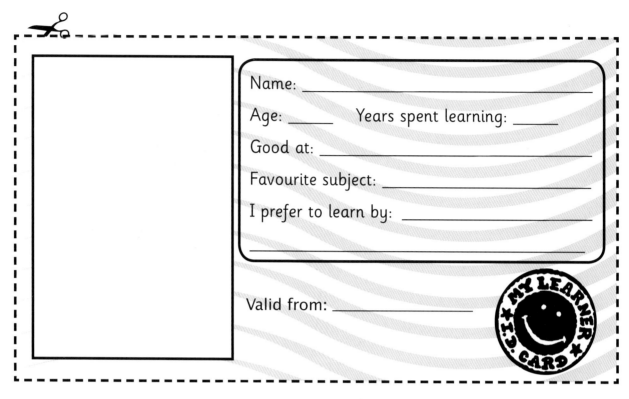

Name: _____

Age: _____   Years spent learning: _____

Good at: _____

Favourite subject: _____

I prefer to learn by: _____

_____

Valid from: _____

MY LEARNER I.D. CARD

Page **24**

- Show what you like best. Put a tick somewhere along each line at the right place for you.

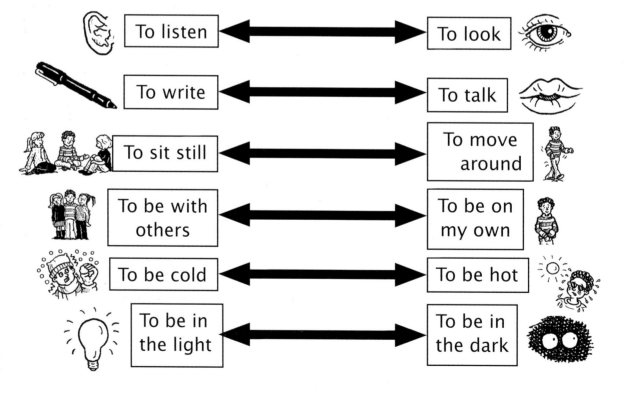

To listen	⟷	To look
To write	⟷	To talk
To sit still	⟷	To move around
To be with others	⟷	To be on my own
To be cold	⟷	To be hot
To be in the light	⟷	To be in the dark

When I'm learning, I prefer_____

Construct a team

Timekeeper

Let everyone know how much time is left.

Leader

Make sure everyone is included.

Talker

Present to the class.

Writer

Do the writing for the team.

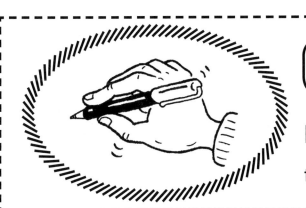

Illustration © 2008, Gemma Hastilow

Learning spies

We want to find:

- _____
- _____
- _____
- _____

We want to hear:

- _____
- _____
- _____
- _____

We want to see:

- _____
- _____
- _____
- _____

■SCHOLASTIC
www.scholastic.co.uk

Chapter Two

Thinking, learning and literacy

- Magic printing machine   28
- Build an author   30
- Freddy's letter home   32
- Journalists' den   34
- Once upon a time   36

This chapter helps you to develop the thinking and learning skills introduced in chapter one, within the context of literacy.

- The first activity, **Magic printing machine**, requires children to practise sentence construction by un-muddling mixed-up sentences. They will also develop teamwork skills by carrying out activities in the 'What to do' section in pairs, and then sharing ideas in groups of four.

- **Build an author** requires children to consider what makes a good author, before they go on to create a 'super author' of their own. They learn facts about different well-known authors and then combine all the different facts and qualities about them to create an author whose book they would like to read.

- In **Freddy's letter home**, children are introduced to letter-writing skills and develop their ability to structure their writing by completing a reordering activity. They also compare and evaluate the advantages and disadvantages of different ways of working: individually, in pairs and in groups. You may want to spend some time looking at letters and their structure in order to get the best out of this activity. Depending on the ages and developmental stage of children in your class, letters may contain emergent writing or writing where high-frequency words are spelled correctly and the rest is phonetically plausible. The activity is designed to be accessible to all children.

- **Journalists' den** introduces the children to newspaper-writing skills, as well as the ability to work under pressure. Children will become aware of the decision-making skills required to produce a newspaper under strict deadlines. Through the activity they also experience working as part of one big team towards a common goal.

- **Once upon a time** requires children to write in a different style and in another genre: this time, direct speech in a fairytale context. They work in small groups to advise Little Red Riding Hood and the three little pigs what to say to the wolf to help him to stop being 'bad'.

Magic printing machine

Setting the context

Sha-ream the engineer is very good at building machines. People from all over the land come to him for help. He builds machines to solve their problems; he builds machines to bath babies; machines to find lost property; machines to make grown-ups fall in love and machines to stop dogs barking. One day an author asks Sha-ream to make a printing machine. The author has forgotten how to use his pen. He needs a machine to suck the thoughts out of his head and print them straight onto paper. Sha-ream makes the machine and the author tries it out. But the words that come out are all muddled. Oh no! The machine is sucking thoughts out in the wrong order!

The challenge

Can you help the author sort out the words from the magic printing machine into sentences that make sense?

Objectives

To be able to solve a problem.
To learn to cooperate with at least one other person.
To be able to construct simple sentences.

You will need

Some muddled sentences of varying type and length (see examples below) for each pair.

Preparation

● To bring this activity to life, you might like to procure items that you could use to create your own magic printing machine – a hoover pipe (for sucking out thoughts from heads) stuck to an old computer which in turn is attached by a wire to a box with a slit in it (for posting through the muddled sentences). Prepare a few muddled sentences on card to demonstrate the machine in action. Choose muddled sentences to match the linguistic abilities of your learners. There are different levels of challenge:

● Sentences where the words need rearranging only:

door open. The is (The door is open.)
door open? the Is (Is the door open?)
ran He away. (He ran away.)

● Two full but muddled sentences:
door open. ran He The away. is (The door is open. He ran away.)

● Sentences without punctuation clues which therefore may have more than one un-muddled version:
door open the is (Is the door open? *or* The door is open.)

● One full sentence with 'decoy' words that won't fit:
door open the is key. (key won't fit unless more words are introduced.

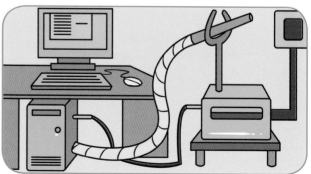

Illustration © 2008, Andy Keylock / Beehive Illustration

● Before you start, copy the 'Levels of success' chart (see below) onto a whiteboard, flipchart or photocopy onto an A4 sheet of paper to refer to when you reach the 'Drawing together' stage.

What to do

● Explain the problem to the children that Sha-ream has invented a magic printing machine for the author but when the words are printed, they come out in the wrong order.

● Demonstrate the machine in action by choosing a child and pretending to 'suck' their thoughts out of their head using the hoover pipe and then showing the muddled sentence that comes out of the machine.

● Challenge the children to discuss with a partner what the real sentence might be.

● Using a whiteboard or flipchart, demonstrate how to un-muddle the sentence.

● Give pairs of children a list of sentences that have come out of the machine and challenge them to un-muddle them.

● Explain that they must work in pairs.

Drawing together

● Arrange the children in fours (two pairs) and ask each pair to discuss with the other pair what they have just been doing, and to choose the sentence that they worked hardest on and explain why it was difficult.

● Repeat for the other pair in the four, but this time ask them to target the easiest sentence. Ask the pairs to share their

Support

● For less confident learners, provide simple, muddled sentences. Short sentences which are punctuated are easier to unscramble.

● You could also make the machine one that removes punctuation only. Challenge children to add it back in to the sentences.

Extension

Extend the activity by using longer sentences, ones without punctuation or ones with decoy words. To challenge the children further, the machine could also muddle up the letters in words, mix up pairs of words and include words with decoy letters. Children then have to un-muddle the letters back into words to make sense of the sentences.

thinking for both the easiest and most difficult sentences. Do they agree?

● Look at the success criteria from the chart and discuss with each pair or four which column they think they are in.

● Suggest other uses for the magic printing machine (printing money by just thinking about it; printing pictures by imagining them and so on) and ask the children to come up with their own new uses for the machine either working in their pairs or as fours.

Levels of success

Not there yet ☆	Nearly there ☆ ☆	Fantastic ☆ ☆ ☆
✔ Some materials used	✔ Most materials used	✔ All materials used
✔ Worked alone	✔ 3 correctly labelled parts	✔ 4 correctly labelled parts
✔ 2 or fewer labelled parts	✔ Finished after 20 minutes	✔ 1 extra labelled part
✔ Not finished yet		✔ Fits in a small shoebox
✔ Bigger than small shoebox		✔ Finished within 20 minutes

Build an author

Setting the context

There are many excellent children's authors at the moment and it's great that you get to read all sorts of different writing – different styles, themes, subjects and formats. For example, Dick King-Smith tells fantastic animal stories; Terry Deary makes history quirky and fun while Nick Butterworth produces cosy and colourful stories and retellings. Each of them, and many others, contribute to a wonderful patchwork of literature.

The challenge

Can you create a new 'super author' by thinking about the characteristics of authors you know and combining them in new ways?

Objectives

To apply structured creative thinking.
To broaden knowledge of the range of literature.
To find out facts about authors' lives and their writing.

You will need

The author body parts template photocopied onto card (see photocopiable page 38); split pins to join the body parts of the author together; author information – see below.

Preparation

● Cut out the pieces from the author templates for children who require this type of support. Select four authors and make sure you have the following information on each one: first and last name, a theme in their writing, their place of birth and an interesting fact. (Information about different authors can be found at: http://www.ukchildrensbooks.co.uk.) Make sure that you have examples of their books to hand. Combine the information into a grid to display on a whiteboard during the activity (see below for an example).

● Make your own author to show the children what they're aiming for. To build a new author, take one item from each row and write it on the appropriate part of the author template from page 38. For example, write your author's first name on the head. On the spare leg, add your own fact, for example, 'likes football', or 'eats no vegetables'. Then

	Bell Mooney	Nick Butterworth	Francesca Simon	Roald Dahl
First Name (head)	Bell	Nick	Francesca	Roald
Last Name (arm)	Mooney	Butterworth	Simon	Dahl
Writes about... (leg)	mischievous little girls	a park-keeper	naughty little boys	strange people and animals
Born in... (arm)	Liverpool	Kingsbury, London	St Louis	Llandaff, Wales
As a child... (body)	always had dirty finger nails in school	lived in a sweet shop	started writing fairy tales, aged 8	kept a secret diary from age 8

join the legs, head and arms to the body with split pins. A finished example could be: Bell Butterworth, born in St Louis, writes about strange people and animals, likes football and lived in a sweet shop as a child. You will also need one large copy or individual copies of the 'Levels of success' chart (see below) to refer to with the children at the end of the activity.

What to do
● Ask the children which authors they have heard of and if they know anything about them.
● Share the information you have gathered on one or two authors who are popular among the children and show some of their books to the class.
● Show the children the author that you built earlier and explain how you made him or her. Show them how to take one fact from each row in the 'author information grid' and explain how this is written on the correct part (head, body, leg or arm) of the author template. Then demonstrate how all the author parts fit together with split pins.
● Tell the children that they can write an extra fact about their author on the spare leg if they want to or they can make up new ideas, rather than taking all their facts from the grid.
● Before they begin, ask pairs of children to explain to each other what to do so everyone is clear about what is required of them.
● Distribute the materials and challenge the children (in groups or individually) to make their own brand new author.

Drawing together
● Display the new authors in the classroom – maybe by pegging them on a washing line or pinning them to a display board
● Ask several children to introduce their author to the rest of the class. They should explain why they have created an author like this. As each one is introduced, ask the class if they would like to read a book by this pretend author.
● Allow children to assess each other's authors against the success criteria from the chart.

Support
For children who may find this activity difficult, prepare some connected authors in advance and add some information to the body parts, showing them where you got your information from and then asking them to fill in the gaps.

Extension
● You could extend this activity further by using an information grid with more rows containing further author facts and even perhaps more authors. Challenge the children to think up possible titles for new books written by the newly-created authors.
● To link with ICT, invite more confident learners to create a mock-up web-page for profiles of new authors.

Page
31

Levels of success

Not there yet ☆	Nearly there ☆☆	Fantastic ☆☆☆
✔ Author has some parts connected together ✔ Some words written on body parts	✔ Author has nearly all parts connected together and moving ✔ Most parts have the right thing written on them	✔ Author has head, body, 2 arms 2 legs that all move ✔ Each part has the right thing written on it ✔ The second leg has a creative fact on it

Freddy's letter home

Setting the context

Meet Freddy Frog! He has dropped into school as part of his tour of Earth. He usually lives in Frogland and this is his first trip away by himself. Actually, he is quietly proud of himself as some strange things have happened to him since he left home. He has been travelling for a while now and he is becoming quite homesick: he misses his family, friends and home. Freddy did keep in contact for a while. He was given a special Frog phone by LeaderFrog before he left for Earth. But the batteries have run out. He would love to write a letter home instead but the pencils we have on Earth are not suitable for his frog feet. So Freddy has a special favour to ask…

The challenge

Can you write a letter for Freddy?

Objectives

To develop knowledge about how to engage in learning.
To know and use the different characteristics of a letter.
To develop confidence, fluency and accuracy in writing, making choices about vocabulary and using phrases and short sentences.

You will need

An outline of a letter from photocopiable page 39, for each child in your class; a pen or pencil; a factsheet of things Freddy would like to include in his letter (use the ideas below or create your own) for each learner or team; a frog puppet to use with the children at the end of the activity (optional).

Preparation

Prepare a table of facts that Freddy would like the children to include in their letters. Photocopy the one from this page or create your own, leaving enough room for the children to add in a number next to each fact. Think about key words that you feel the children will need to have displayed in order

Freddy would like you to include the following information:

favourite food	miss you	visiting a school
Dear Froggies	friends	frog phone
?	pencil	Love Freddy

to write their letter. It will also be helpful if you have talked with the children in a previous lesson about how we learn. Completing the 'Learner identity cards' activity on page 12 will introduce children to the right concepts and ideas.

What to do
● Explain the scenario to the children and invite them to ask questions about Freddy Frog.
● Discuss with the children how they learn and look at their Learner ID cards if they have completed the activity on page 12. Focus on the section of the card that shows whether they like to learn alone or with a group of children.
● Encourage the children to decide how they want to work on this activity: alone, with a partner, with a group of three or with a large group (possibly supported by an adult). You may also want to offer a variety of different learning spaces – a single table, a group of tables, floor space, lights off in one area and on in another and so on.
● Introduce the things that Freddy would like the children to include in his letter. Discuss what the words and pictures might mean. What do they think Freddy means by leaving a question mark in one of the boxes? Can they think of questions that Freddy might want to ask his friends and family at home. Which order do the children think the facts should be placed? Ask them to show the order by putting numbers in the boxes.
● Ask the children to tell each other what they have to do and then ask them to tell you what they have to do. Invite the children to indicate their level of understanding of the task, for example, by standing up if they are ready to start, by putting their hands on their heads if they are not quite sure but want to begin and check again later or sitting on their hands if they want to check something out again.
● Lastly, ask the children to think about 'what makes a letter a letter?' *What should a letter look like?* Write the children's ideas down in a visible list – perhaps accompanied by a sketch.
● Tell the children that they have 30

minutes to write the letter for Freddy.
● Remind the children of any class routines you already have for writing, for example, using word cards/word books.
● Establish some success criteria as a class: what do the children think they need to do to reach three stars?

Drawing together
● Invite Freddy Frog to come and listen to the letters and encourage the children to read their letters aloud to him.
● Use Freddy Frog to say what he liked about each letter, highlighting letter structure and content of the facts included.
● Ask the children what they liked about their letters and what they would do differently if they had five minutes extra. Then allow five minutes extra for the improvements to be made.
● Talk about the learning experience with the class. *Would it be good to learn alone all the time? Is it good to always work with others? Was it easier or harder to do a writing activity alone or with others? Why?*

Support
● Provide key words on a display and include some sentence starters for Freddy's letter to help children who may have difficulty with the activity.
● Simplify the task by reducing the number of facts the children need to include in their letters.

Extension
● Make use of ICT by allowing the children to record themselves reading their letters aloud or let them write their letters on the computer. Add a design and technology angle by challenging the children to make envelopes for the letters.
● Extend the task further by arranging for the children to receive a letter from Frogland in reply.

Journalists' den

Setting the context

Your classroom has become a 'journalists' den'. I am Penny (or Paul) Paperclip – one of the directors in charge of the office and you are my office workers. The first job that we have to do is to make a newspaper about our office. The 'Big Boss', Sir Hardnose, is coming to visit tomorrow and he is expecting to see a copy of the first edition of the newspaper which will tell him a little bit about every member of staff. For each office worker there must be a newspaper article which includes a picture, graphics or a photo, a heading and some information about who you are and what you like or don't like.

The challenge

Can you create a newspaper by the end of the day?

Objectives

To develop decision-making skills.
To work independently towards a large group product using self-motivation and perseverance.
To learn how to use a checklist during an activity.
To reflect on the learning process.

You will need

A copy of the layout for one page of the newspaper from photocopiable page 40, for each child; pencils; badges showing the different roles in the office (office worker, Assistant Director, IT team) from photocopiable page 41. The Assistant Director will need a timer, a notepad and a pen. The IT team will need a computer and a printer. You will also need to organise the space in the classroom to include a Publishing Area which offers safe access to pairs of scissors and glue and A3 sheets of card already stapled together to form a newspaper. You may want to cover the front and back in real newspaper, to add some authenticity. You will also need a Graphics Area which will also require safe access to pairs of scissors Thind glue; a photo of each child and paper for illustrations to be drawn on. You will also need a visible way to count down 45 minutes such as a classroom clock or sand timer. (Use a teaching clock to show the end time and demonstrate how to watch the classroom clock move towards this time.)

Preparation

● Rearrange your classroom into an office space, for example, individual desks in rows, four chairs in a circle with a coffee table in the middle for breaks, a graphics table and a publishing table with appropriate resources. Photocopy and cut out the badges. Make sure that you have sticky tape ready to attach them to the children.
● Prepare the 'Levels of success' chart (see page 35) to refer during the activity.

What to do

● Explain the scenario to the children and let them ask questions about the office.
● Appoint children with the office roles, give out the badges and explain the different roles. The Assistant Director helps to run the office (appoint a child who will be confident enough to speak in front of the class, but less confident at attempting writing tasks). He or she checks everyone is working, helps out and answers questions, keeps the time, allows coffee breaks and reports to you, the Director. The IT team designs the title for the newspaper. Assign the rest of the children roles as office workers.

Photograph © 2008, JupiterImage Corporation

● Display the 'Levels of success' chart. Explain that Sir Hardnose has already sent a list with what he expects to be in the newspaper – but that the children could impress him more by adding extra detail in the 'Could' section. Ask the children to think of additional information that could be included and add their ideas to the 'Could' section.

● Make sure that the success criteria is on display and easily accessible during the task. Remind the children that they can use the list at any time.

● Tell them that they will have only 45 minutes to create their newspaper article about themselves and make the whole newspaper. Show the children the newspaper format they have to complete. Let them ask questions to clarify their understanding.

● Ask the Assistant Director to read the office rules (see photocopiable page 41).

● Tell the workers that the office is now open and that they have 45 minutes to finish their articles.

Drawing together

● Ask the children to look at their newspaper articles and reflect on how well they have met the criteria that were set.

● Have each team to think of one thing they would add if they had an extra five minutes. Allow the teams to amend or add to their newspaper articles, within the five minutes.

● Organise for someone to dress up as Sir Hardnose and visit the class to look at the newspaper and ask questions about what it was like working in an office. He or she should assess the newspaper according to the success criteria from the chart.

Illustration © 2008, Andy Keylock / Beehive Illustration

Support
● Limit the resources or extend the time allowed to complete the task.
● Provide key words or scaffold sentences to help less confident learners.

Extension
● The children could become reporters and interview other members of the school or they could make a follow-up newspaper about a particular issue.
● Some office workers could write pages on behalf the IT team and the Assistant Director to ensure that everyone in the class is represented in the newspaper. This could also involve some interview work.

Levels of success

Must ☆	Should ☆☆	Could ☆☆☆
✔ Write your name ✔ Add your photo ✔ Write your age	✔ Write about what you like ✔ Write about what you don't like	

Once upon a time

Setting the context
Ever since she had experienced difficulties with a nasty wolf in the forest, Little Red Riding Hood always stayed on the pathways. One day, she took a different path. She was on her way to town when she came upon a house made of bricks with three little pigs playing in the garden. The pigs noticed her and invited her to have a drink of dandelion tea. As Little Red Riding Hood was thirsty, she immediately said, 'Yes, please'. The pigs and Little Red Riding Hood got on very well and were soon exchanging funny stories and scary ones too! That's when they realised that they had all experienced problems with the same wolf! 'I think we should do something about this,' said Little Red Riding Hood. 'I'm sure we can persuade him to stop being so nasty. Let's think of some things we could say to him.'

The challenge
What can you say to the wolf to help him become kind? Write down your ideas and send them via special mail to Fairytale Land. The last post goes at 7pm.

Objectives
To work collaboratively within strict time limits.
To evaluate the impact of new thoughts.
To develop writing skills using speech bubbles or speech marks.

You will need
A pencil and three pieces of card or paper for each team; glue; safe access to pairs of scissors. You could use a copy of the map on photocopiable page 42. You will also need a visible way to count down time such as a classroom clock or a sand timer. (Use a teaching clock to show the end time. Show the children how to watch the classroom clock move towards this time.)

Photograph © 2008, Scholastic Ltd

Preparation

The children will need to have already had some experience of writing speech either using speech bubbles or speech marks. They will also need to be familiar with the stories of the Three Little Pigs and Little Red Riding Hood.

What to do

● Divide the children into groups of three.
● Introduce the scenario, using the map on photocopiable page 42 and invite the children to ask questions about the task.
● Establish the requirements of the activity and some success criteria, such as:

1. You must think of things to say that will persuade the wolf to become kind.
2. You must record these on paper or card.
3. You may choose to use a speech bubble or speech marks.
4. You must agree your choices with your team and finish within 30 minutes.

● Give the children an opportunity to clarify their understanding with you, for example, by answering questions such as: *What are speech bubbles?; What are speech marks?*
● Tell them that they will be working together and what this should look like and sound like (listening to each other, sharing ideas, making joint decisions, no shouting, and so on).

Drawing together

● Ask the learners to look at their finished ideas and assess how well they have met the criteria that were set. Allow time for the children to alter any writing to ensure that speech marks are correctly placed.
● Ask learners to read out their ideas to each other and encourage them to ask questions about each other's ideas.
● Ask questions about how the teams worked together. The children should consider what they did well and what they would do differently next time.
● Remind the teams to listen to everyone's ideas about what to say and then choose the top three ideas to record.
● Dress up as Little Red Riding Hood or send a letter from her explaining to the children how their ideas for the wolf worked.

"Hello Mr Wolf. Don't be mean all the time. Be nice to pigs!"

"But I don't know how to be nice."

"Don't show your teeth or growl at people. Be friendly and help other people. Then people will like you."

"Ok. I will try."

"Thanks!"

Page
37

Support
● Allow more time or organise groups carefully to allow the children to support each other.
● Provide examples of speech bubbles or speech marks.

Extension
Develop speech into role-play scenarios.

Build an author

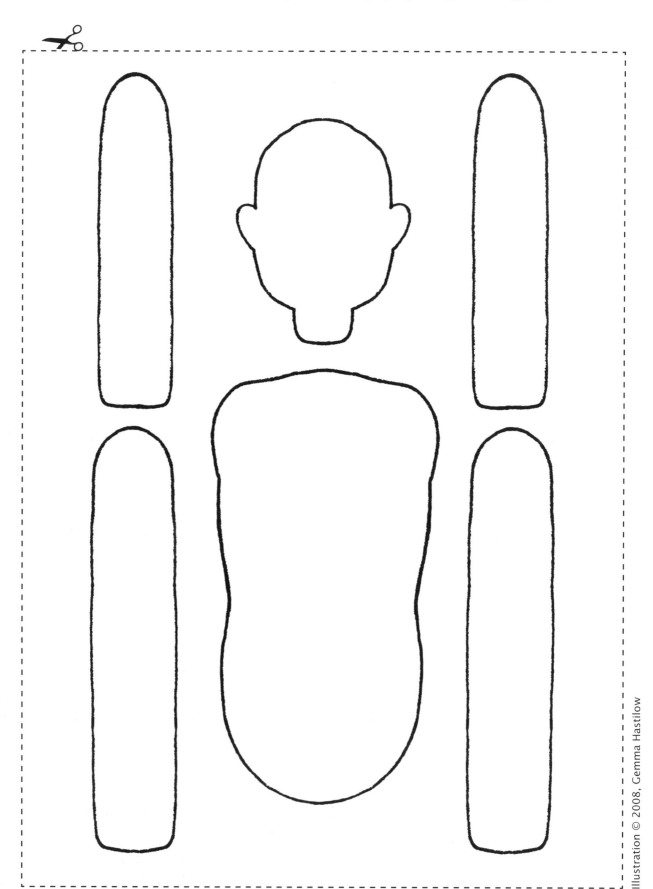

Freddy's letter

● Write a letter for Freddy.

_____

_____

_____

_____

_____

_____

_____

_____

_____

_____

_____

_____

_____

_____

■SCHOLASTIC
www.scholastic.co.uk

Creative Activities for Thinking and Learning Skills: Ages 5-7

Journalists' den (1)

Photo

Photo

Photo

■SCHOLASTIC
www.scholastic.co.uk

Journalists' den (2)

Rules for the office

1. You must ask the Assistant Director if you want to leave your workspace.
2. You are allowed a 2 minute coffee break when the Assistant Director says it is your turn.
3. You are allowed to ask for help.
4. It is your responsibility to get your article finished.
5. Use the checklist to make sure you have done everything.

Assistant Director

Office worker

I.T. team

■SCHOLASTIC
www.scholastic.co.uk
PHOTOCOPIABLE Creative Activities for Thinking and Learning Skills: Ages 5-7

Once upon a time

SCHOLASTIC
www.scholastic.co.uk

Chapter Three

Thinking, learning, numeracy and science

- Alien number abduction 44
- Shape Land people   46
- Celebrate with me   48
- The number worm   50
- Multi-coloured lab coat 52

In this chapter children develop their thinking and learning skills within the contexts of numeracy and science.

● In **Alien number abduction**, children help aliens to sort numbers according to different criteria: numbers below 20, even numbers, numbers in the five-times table and so on. The aliens then use their 'Vooverator' to send these numbers back home. Children at Key Stage 1 have a very wide range of mathematical ability and meeting all their needs with one activity is an interesting challenge. Activities that allow children of different abilities to collaborate on the same task, have many benefits such as, raising mathematical esteem, developing problem-solving skills alongside maths and more meaningful and engaging teaching and learning.

● **Shape Land people** is set in the imaginary world of Shape Land and it provides the children with an opportunity to explore and investigate 2D shapes. The children work in teams to make a picture of a person from Shape Land, using a variety of shapes and they explore which shapes are most useful when trying to create the person's body. In the Extension activity, the children respond to a letter from the Shape Land mayor and determine the best shape to use to construct a straight road, without any bumps or potholes (gaps). Both activities develop the children's knowledge of the names and the properties of 2D shapes.

● In **Celebrate with me**, children make paper chains for a birthday party. They work in teams to build the longest chain possible, with a repeating pattern, in a short amount of time.

● **The number worm** requires children to solve simple maths problems in teams of three. The task is to rid the beach of the largest number worms – those that eat the most numbers. The children need to solve the maths problems to work out, for example, whether a worm that eats all even numbers eats less numbers than a worm that only eats numbers in the three-times table?

● In **Multi-coloured lab coat**, children contribute to the creation of a decorated class lab coat. The decorations are inspired by maths topics and maths thinking. Individuals, pairs or small groups each contribute a piece of the coat.

Alien number abduction

Setting the context

Aliens are visiting us to find out more about Earth. You and your team are helping them by collecting the things that they want to look at, but there's a problem. The aliens are so ugly and smelly that humans cannot go anywhere near them. So the aliens are using a 'Vooverator'. This is a machine which snatches things away from great distances. Your team puts things onto a special 'Vooverator Pad', then the aliens switch on the Vooverator and the things disappear, whizzing straight into the aliens' spaceship.

The challenge

This week, the aliens are collecting numbers with their Vooverator. Your job is to put the right numbers on the Vooverator Pad before the aliens switch it on.

Photograph © 2008, JupiterImages Corporation

Objectives

To assume a specific role within a team.
To develop planning, monitoring and evaluation skills.
To be able to sort specific numbers using criteria such as 'greater than', 'odd', 'in the 2x times table'.

You will need

Some small 1–100 number cards (see photocopiable page 54) and some Blu-Tack® for each team. You will also need a 'Vooverator' – use a suitable, clean vacuum cleaner with the dust collection bag disconnected (whatever the machine sucks up, it will need to come out before entering the bag) and a piece of card to make the 'Vooverator Pad'.

Preparation

Test the Vooverator (vacuum cleaner as above) and Vooverator Pad (a piece of card, add alien decoration if you wish). If you or another adult wishes to dress up as an alien, gather suitable attire beforehand.

What to do

● Arrange the children into teams of varying mathematical ability.
● Allocate the following jobs: the children can be in teams of fours, or in pairs with each person doing two jobs:
    1. Number Picker (selects the 'right' numbers from the pile).
    2. Blu-Tack® Manager (fixes small pieces of Blu-Tack® to the remaining numbers).
    3. Number Sticker (places the chosen 'right' numbers and sticks the remaining numbers to the Vooverator Pad).
    4. Pad Checker (does a final check to make sure that the numbers the aliens don't want are stuck down and that those they do want are not stuck down.
● Explain and present the problem to the children: The aliens want even numbers from

1–20. Stick 1,3,5,7,9,11,13,15,17,19 to the pad and place the even numbers there too (unstuck). Switch on the Vooverator so that it sucks up the even numbers. After 'Vooveration', collect the Vooverated numbers and ask the children to check that the even numbers have been sucked up.

● Then, set appropriate Vooveration number challenges for each team. For example: greater than 10; less than 15; even numbers; odd numbers; in the 2x table; in the 2x and 5x tables; numbers with a curve; numbers with one syllable; numbers greater than 20 when doubled.

● Ask the children to prepare their pads then bring them to you for Vooveration. After Vooveration, collect the Vooverated numbers and ask pairs of teams to check each other's work.

● Ask the children to change jobs where possible and encourage all group members to be involved in the solving of the problem each time.

Drawing together

● Ask the teams, taking each role in turn, to say one easy and one difficult thing about the job that they did.

● Ask the teams to comment on checking each other's work.

● Can each team decide on one thing they would do differently next time to make the work easier?

Support

● Group less confident learners with those who can help them with mathematical collaborative skills.

● Adapt the Vooverator criteria, for example, the aliens want numbers less than 5 (from 1–10) instead of less than 10 (from 1–20). Allow more time and provide adult support.

Extension

● Set two or more criteria and have two or more Vooverators and pads. The 'suckings' of the first Vooverator are stuck or sucked up by the second.

● Set more challenging Vooverator criteria, such as, prime numbers less than 100. Allow teams to set their own criteria or determine criteria for other groups.

Page
45

Illustration © 2008, Andy Keylock / Beehive Illustration

Creative Activities for Thinking and Learning Skills: Ages 5-7

Shape Land people

Photograph © 2008, Lynne Williams

Setting the context

You are explorers about to enter a new land. It seems like you've been climbing for ages but you're near the top now and the hatch is just above you. You turn around and whisper to your friends, 'We're here. We must be quiet... we don't want to scare whoever is through the hatch'. Your team nod back. You all get ready to gently push the hatch upwards. You gasp in amazement. It is the most peculiar land so far. A land of shapes! You can't believe your eyes... and then you realise that everything is 2D! It's so strange that you decide to take a photo. You reach for your camera... but it's not there! It must have fallen out! Thinking quickly, you realise that your memory can take a picture. You all look around, studying the shape people, trying hard to remember all the shapes that make up their bodies. You can't wait to get back to start your picture!

The challenge

Can you make a picture of a shape person? You need to work as a team and use each other's memories to think about the 'shape person' you saw.

Objectives

To work collaboratively to create a solution to a problem.
To use decision-making skills.
To know the names of 2D shapes and some of their properties.

You will need

Scrap paper or small whiteboards and pens; copies of photocopiable page 55; large sheets of card; prepared packs of 2D shape templates made from a variety of materials for children to use in their pictures and/or a selection of 2D shapes for them to draw around – circles, rectangles, squares, triangles, stars, octagons, pentagons, semi-circles, ovals, diamonds and hexagons; access to coloured paper and card, glitter, wool, wobbly eyes and other decorations for the 'surprise element'; safe access to pairs of scissors and glue; shape labels or a list with spellings of 2D shape names. You could also use photocopiable page 56 for the Extension.

Preparation

Before the session, photocopy the checklist and shape labels from page 55. Prepare 2D shape templates of different colours/textures and make up a pack for each team. Children will need to be prepared for entering the scenario through extended experience of role play. You could engage your class in a variety of preparatory experiences, including, climbing up apparatus (imaginary trees), visualising familiar places such as a local park, the town or a place of interest – describing the sights and sounds: *What can you see? What can you hear? Who are you with?* Then move on to less familiar places

Photograph © 2008, Lynne Williams

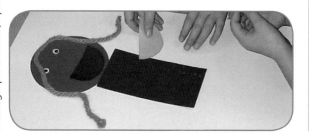

such as a jungle, desert or farm. Prepare the 'Levels of success' chart (see below) to refer to during the activity.

What to do
● Organise the children into teams of three in preparation for a role-play activity.
● Lead the teams through the scenario outlined above using movement, expression and possibly 'freeze-frame' questioning, for example, *What shape legs can you see?*
● Allow the teams a short time for discussion to explore/brainstorm the shape people they have visualised. The teams can then record their ideas on whiteboards/paper and report back. They should decide on one shape person they will create together.
● Display the success criteria and explore what a successful picture of a shape person would look like.
● Introduce and the 'checklist' of body parts and discuss how the teams could use this while they are working.
● Discuss what 'working together' would look like and sound like. Record and display the children's ideas in words and pictures.
● Send the groups to their tables and ask each group to nominate someone to collect their resources – a large sheet of card, a bag of shape templates and/or 2D shapes.
● Tell them that they have 20 minutes to create and label their picture. Start the timer or show them the end time on the 'teaching clock' just before they begin.
● Once each group has completed their picture, invite them to present their 'shape person' to the rest of the class. Alternatively the groups could swap pictures and identify or count the shapes used.

Drawing together
● Ask questions such as: *Did your team work together well? What happened if you disagreed about which shapes to use?*
● Encourage the children to think about what they would do differently next time.
● Find out which shape was used the most/ least. *Why?* Ask the children what they have learned about shapes.

Support
Ensure that copies of the checklist are provided for the children to use.

Extension
Carry out an investigation to find out which 2D shape could be used to construct a 'good' road. Read the letter from the Shape Land mayor (see page 56) and then explore the qualities of a 'good' road – straight, smooth, without any bumps. Each group could build three roads, using the 2D shape templates and card. Ask the groups to order their roads, from the bumpiest to the smoothest (a bumpy road would have gaps between shapes). Once they have decided which shape is best, each group could present their findings and explain their choices.

Levels of success

Not yet ☆	Nearly there ☆☆	Fantastic ☆☆☆
✔ Shapes in the wrong order – like 2 arms on one side	✔ Some shapes in right place, some in wrong	✔ All shapes in right place so 1 arm on each side
✔ Labels upside down, not in right place, wobbly, wonky or not used	✔ Some labels in right place, some not, some cut through the middle	✔ All labels are in right place
	✔ There is a surprise – but it is wobbly	✔ Surprise is interesting

Celebrate with me

Photograph © 2008, JupiterImages Corporation

Setting the context

It's Molly's mum's 30th birthday soon. Molly wants to make this birthday really special but she wants it to be a surprise. She doesn't have anyone else to help her as her grandparents live quite a long way away. Molly's mum is in a wheelchair and Molly knows that her mum would love to be able to touch all the pretty decorations that she makes, so they need to be as long as possible when they are hanging down from the ceiling. Molly has discovered that you know all about making paper chains. She has sent along a package full of resources. There are enough squares of gummed paper for each group to choose two colours and have at least three sheets of each colour.

The challenge

Can you help Molly make some paper chains? They need to be long, with a repeating pattern, as Molly's mum loves patterns. Molly will pick them up at lunchtime.

Objectives

To learn to work creatively and collaboratively within strict time limits and with limited resources.
To investigate repeating patterns using shapes.

You will need

Pencils; sheets of coloured gummed paper 20cm x 20cm; plastic dishes; copies of photocopiable page 57; glue; safe access to pairs of scissors; a variety of standard and non-standard measuring apparatus. You will also need a visible way to count down 20 minutes such as a classroom clock or a sand timer. You could use a teaching clock to show the end time. Show the children how to watch the classroom clock move towards this time.

Preparation

As part of the introduction or as a separate session, you may want to explore with the children what a paper chain is. This could be a research question for a homework task, or you could introduce it as an investigative activity where the children predict what paper chains are or identify the most likely choice from a group of pictures. Children will also need to have had prior experience of repeating patterns and measurement. Before you begin this activity, gather the required materials together and place them in plastic dishes on each groups' table or in a central resource zone.

What to do

● Divide the class into groups of three.
● Read the scenario to the children and encourage them to ask questions about Molly.
● Point out the requirements of the task and the success criteria:
   1. You must use all of your resources – nothing can be left over.
   2. Your paper chain must be a repeating pattern.
   3. Your paper chain must be as long

Photograph © 2008, Andrea Lewis

as possible.

4. Your paper chain must only have two colours.

5. You must make it with your team and finish within 20 minutes.

● Ask the children to explain to a partner what Molly has asked them all to do. Give them an opportunity to clarify their understanding with you by answering questions such as: *What are paper chains? What is a repeating pattern?*

● Tell them that they will have only 20 minutes to make their paper chain before it is time for Molly to collect them.

● Explain to the children that they will be working together and ask them what they think this will look like and sound like. Ask them to consider the best way to work as a team to produce the longest paper chain in a small amount of time.

Drawing together

● Ask the learners to look at their finished paper chains and assess how well they have met the criteria that were set in the checklist.

● How could they measure their paper chains? Discuss as a class what happens if

each team uses a different form of measurement.

● Encourage children to ask questions about each other's paper chain. *Why are some longer when they all started with the same amount of paper?*

● Ask questions about how teams worked together, such as: *What did you do well? What would you do differently next time?*

Support

Extend the amount of time allowed or adapt the success criteria to make the activity more achievable for less confident learners. Keep everyone on task by creating and referring to a checklist throughout the activity.

Extension

Can the children order all of the paper chains made as a class from longest to shortest? Choose a suitable form of measurement and create a chart to represent the data.

The number worm

Photograph © 2008, JupiterImages Corporation

Setting the context

When the tide goes out, a beach is often covered with curly worm-casts. As the worms burrow into the sand they eat it, taking what nourishment they can from it and letting the rest pass right the way through – hence the wormy shapes left on the surface. A number worm does exactly the same thing except that it eats numbers, but only certain numbers. Number worms are taking over the beach and are making it difficult for holidaymakers to enjoy their time at the seaside. Some number worms are worse than others and it is your job to find these, dig them up and take them to another beach.

The challenge

How many problem number worms can you find? Work in teams of three with a spotter, a tester and an examiner. You will only catch the worms if you cooperate.

Objectives

To learn to work cooperatively in a team of three, within a specific role.
To explore basic number operations.
To evaluate group performance and set targets for improvement.

You will need

An image or video clip of worm-casts – perhaps even real worms; copies of photocopiable page 58; a name badge or label for each child depending on whether they are a spotter (chooses the worms), a tester (puts the numbers into the worms), or an examiner (looks at the casts).

Preparation

Decide how you are going to describe the creation of worm-casts to the children and prepare the necessary materials. Prepare a number worm sheet to suit the mathematical abilities of your learners; use the sheet as supplied or make copies of the final row and then add in your own text. Prepare the role badges. Make copies of the 'Levels of success' chart for the children to refer to at the end of the activity.

What to do

● Present the idea of worm-casts to the children and explain that a number worm

Illustration © 2008, Andy Keylock / Beehive Illustration

eats certain numbers, but lets the rest pass through to make a worm-cast.

● Demonstrate a simple number worm eating up numbers larger than 10 (use numbers 1–20), but letting the rest pass through into the cast.

● Tell the children that they are going to work as a team of three to catch number worms. Each person has a role and a badge: the Spotter chooses which worm to investigate and decides whether the worm is a big problem (has eaten a lot of numbers) and needs to be taken to a different beach; the Tester puts numbers into the worm (writes the numbers into the final column on the worksheet); the Examiner examines the worm-cast (checks that the answers on the worksheet are correct).

● Arrange the children into teams of three and allocate the different roles.

● Work through one example from the number worm worksheet on page 58 and

remind the children of their roles and how important it is to the success of the task to keep to their team roles.

● Distribute copies of the number worm worksheets (one for each team) and begin learning.

Drawing together

● Call the teams back together and ask them to share their findings

● Prompt them to think about their teamwork and to assess themselves using the success criteria from the chart below.

● Ask each team to decide on one thing that they were really proud of in their task and one thing that they would like to do better next time.

Support
You could adapt the number worms to make the number problems easier and arrange for adult support if necessary.

Extension
Fill the 'sand' with larger numbers or provide more complex number worms and challenge the children to create and examine the new worms. Increase the team sizes to four and add a tide watcher, limiting the time to complete the task. Repeat the task and expect the target for improvement to occur in the same lesson.

Levels of success

Must ☆	Should ☆☆	Could ☆☆☆
✔ No one did their job	✔ 2 people did their jobs	✔ Everyone did their job
✔ No worms were investigated	✔ Most worms were investigated	✔ All worms were investigated
✔ The team argued	✔ There was a bit of disagreement	✔ Everyone helped each other

Multi-coloured lab coat

Setting the context
Professor Hypoth is being teased by his fellow scientists. They all have cool and trendy lab coats in which to perform their experiments but the Professor is still wearing the grubby old white one which was given to him when he started work. The only things on his coat are spilled chemicals and dirty handprints. But help is at hand. Professor Hypoth has asked a team of designers to decorate his coat, from collar to hem, with bright and colourful images and words – all about the world of maths.

The challenge
Can you decorate part of the Professor's lab coat? When all of the parts have been completed, put them together to produce the new lab coat.

Objectives
To explore different ways of working: individually, with a partner, or in a small group.
To be able to describe a maths or science idea by drawing a single image and in less than five words.

You will need
A real lab coat for demonstration; two large pieces of paper or card (A1 size); some resource materials for ideas, such as, science books, websites, posters or equipment; copies of the 'Levels of success' chart for the children to use at the end of the activity.

Preparation
Draw a lab coat shape onto one large piece of card (or paper), cut it out and then use it as a template to draw around on the other piece of card. Split one of the card lab coats into sections of differing sizes and cut out

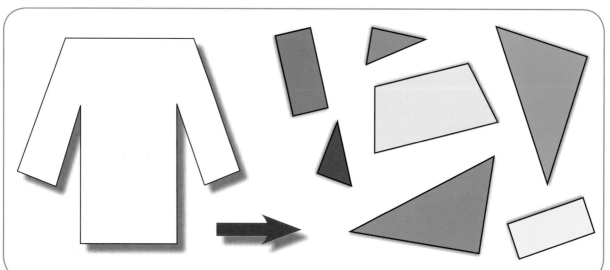

the pieces so that they can be put back together like a jigsaw. Prepare an example piece for the coat, meeting the success criteria set out below, to show to the children.

What to do
● Describe the problem to the children and explain that they have been challenged to make a multi-coloured, science, lab coat for Professor Hypoth.
● Show them a real lab coat, perhaps by wearing one or allowing some of the children to try one on. Then, show them the card lab coat and the pieces that will fit together to make it.
● Each piece of coat must adhere to the following rules. It must:
    1. be completely covered.
    2. have one picture from the world of science (drawn, printed or cut out from a magazine) on it.
    3. have between three and five words describing the picture.
    4. have at least three colours.
● Ask the children to think about whether they would like to work on their own, with a partner or in a small group of three or four children.
● Let them choose how to work and organise them accordingly. Then, distribute the materials and allow them to begin the task.

Drawing together
● As the children finish their pieces, assemble them onto the lab coat outline

on the second large piece of card.
● Ask the children to assess each other's work using the success criteria from the chart below to help them. On their copy of the chart, ask them to tick the criteria which they think have been met and then ask them to decide overall if the piece of lab coat deserves one, two or three stars.

Support
● Provide a maths image bank and an associated wordbank to offer suggestions for what the children can put on their pieces of lab coat.
● Limit the choice of how to work, for example, by organising the children into pairs and making sure you pair up less confident learners with those who will be competent at the task.
● Give out smaller pieces of card for the children to cover. In this way, the task will be less time-consuming.

Extension
● Develop criteria for multi-coloured uniforms for other professions, such as the police, fire service, mechanics, musicians and so on and invite the children to make new card clothing.
● Ask them to work in a different way next time so they can compare how they worked individually with working in pairs or a group.

Levels of success

Not there yet ☆	Nearly there ☆☆	Fantastic ☆☆☆
✔ Big border around picture	✔ Most of the card covered	✔ 1 or 2 colours
✔ No words	✔ 1 picture	✔ 1 picture about science
✔ No colour	✔ 1, 2 or more than 5 words	✔ 3, 4 or 5 words
	✔ 1 or 2 colours	✔ 3 or more colours

Alien number abduction

1	2	3	4	5	6	7	8	9	10
11	12	13	14	15	16	17	18	19	20
21	22	23	24	25	26	27	28	29	30
31	32	33	34	35	36	37	38	39	40
41	42	43	44	45	46	47	48	49	50
51	52	53	54	55	56	57	58	59	60
61	62	63	64	65	66	67	68	69	70
71	72	73	74	75	76	77	78	79	80
81	82	83	84	85	86	87	88	89	90
91	92	93	94	95	96	97	98	99	100

Shape Land people

● Make sure your shape person has the following body parts:

2 arms	1 body
1 head	2 eyes
2 legs	1 nose
2 hands	1 mouth
2 feet	1 surprise!

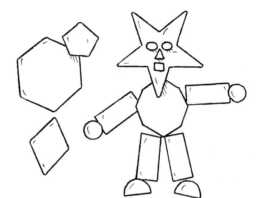

● Add labels to your shape person:

Page 55

square	rectangle
circle	pentagon
octagon	hexagon
triangle	semi-circle
star	oval
diamond	

Illustration © 2008, Gemma Hastilow

Shape Land letter

Dear 'Hatch Peekers',

You may not know this but our cameras caught you looking into our land! We don't mind having visitors...in fact we were really pleased that someone new decided to stop by. You may be able to help us with a problem!

We really could do with some help. A big argument is about to break out in Shape Land. A month ago the mayor received some money from an anonymous person. He decided that we could use the money to build a road from the village to the 'Park of Diamonds' – at the moment there is only a muddy track. So if it rains we get all dirty.

However, the mayor wanted us all to have the opportunity to give our ideas. THIS IS WHEN THE PROBLEM BEGAN.

Cyril said the road should be made of circles
Rodney said it should be made of rectangles
Squiffy said it should be made of squares
Trinny said it should be made of triangles
Stef said it should be made of stars
Petula said it should be made of pentagons
Semolina said it should be made of semi-circles
Harold said it should be made of hexagons.

The mayor is now in a dilemma because all the shape people are arguing. He doesn't know which idea to use and he really doesn't want to upset anyone.

Can you help in anyway?

Yours sincerely,

Diamond Geezer

The Deputy Mayor.

SCHOLASTIC
www.scholastic.co.uk

This is Molly

- This is Molly.

- Molly wants to make her mum's birthday special. She wants to make some paper chains to hang up. Please can you help her?

- They must have:

  1. 2 colours

  2. a repeating pattern

  3. and they must be as long as possible.

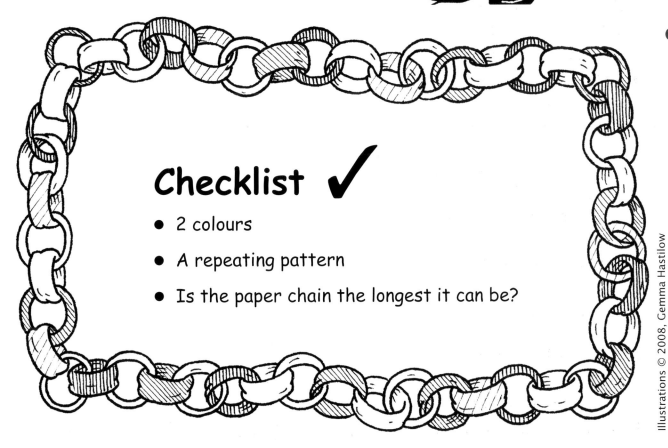

Checklist ✔

- 2 colours

- A repeating pattern

- Is the paper chain the longest it can be?

Illustrations © 2008, Gemma Hastilow

SCHOLASTIC
www.scholastic.co.uk

The number worm

Chapter Four

Thinking, learning and the humanities

- You're history   60
- Time traveller   62
- Pirate islands   64

The three activities in this chapter allow children to practise and improve their thinking and learning skills in the context of history and geography.

● **You're history** combines historical characters and events with children's self-knowledge as learners. It can be used at the end of a history topic you are studying or as soon as the children have a working knowledge of their own learning and thinking skills (see the Le Fevre Teaching Board activity on pages 20–21). The activity refers to topic work based around the Romans but it can be used to consolidate knowledge of any history topic. Children are required to think about what skills they possess that would help them survive in a historical setting.

● **Time traveller** continues the theme of travelling back into the past. In this activity, children help Dr Brown to identify appropriate questions to use when travelling back in time. Children develop their skills of historical enquiry and learn that when finding out about the past they will learn more effectively and can be more productive in their answers and interpretations if they ask the right questions. They have to decide which questions are good ones to ask. For young learners, this will probably be rooted initially in what interests them. It will not be about what they 'should' know, but more about what they 'want' to know.

● In **Pirate islands**, children work in groups to prepare a map of a treasure island for Captain Pegleg and his crew. They need to consider the essential features that every map should have and create their own assessment criteria as a class. At the end of the activity, Captain Pegleg looks at the maps and helps the children evaluate how well they have met the criteria they set themselves at the beginning of the task as well as how well they worked together as a team.

You're history

Setting the context
It can be hard to work out what happened in the distant past: there are no photos, videos or audio clips and no people left to tell us about it. Wouldn't it be great to live in those times shown in the history books so that we could find out for ourselves what it was like? But if we really did manage to travel back in time, would we have the skills to survive?

The challenge
We know a lot about the Romans and a lot about our learning and thinking skills. Can you use this knowledge to survive life in Roman times?

Objectives
To further develop self-knowledge as a learner.
To think, learn and work independently.
To consolidate knowledge and understanding of a historical topic.

You will need
A copy of photocopiable page 66 for each child; a plastic, games hoop.

Preparation
Make sure that the children have free access to work produced during their study of the history topic on the Romans, as well as access to source materials previously used in the topic. They should also be able to refer to a record of knowledge for their thinking and learning skills (such as a learning mat or a Le Fevre teaching board).

What to do
● Explain to the children that they will be going backwards in time through the time hoop.
● Describe the point in history to which you want them to travel, in order to set the scene, for example, the Romans landing on British shores; Boudicca assembling an army.
● Ask the children to complete the two statements at the beginning of photocopiable page 66.
● Tell them that before they go travelling back in time, you need to check that they will have the skills to survive. Ask them to think about and then complete the skills checklist on their worksheets. Show them how to mark each of the six skills with a cross, somewhere on the line between 'Yes' and 'No', depending on how good they think they are at each skill.
● Then invite the children to step back

Illustration © 2008, Andy Keylock / Beehive Illustration

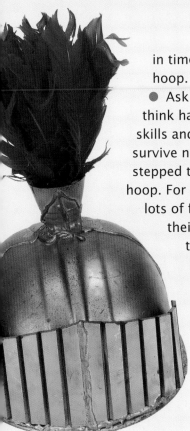

in time through the hoop.

● Ask the children to think hard about their skills and how they might survive now that they have stepped through the time hoop. For example, 'knowing lots of facts' will help in their understanding of the historical period and will also help when trying to fit in with the people; being good at thinking up 'new ideas' (creative thinking) could help in advising famous characters from the past when they are trying to solve a particular problem.

● Ask the children to consider the prompts at the bottom of the photocopiable page 66 and encourage them to write down their own thoughts about the skills they possess.

Drawing together

● Bring the children back together by asking them to step back into the present, through the time hoop.

● Step through the time hoop yourself and model the sharing of your skills and how they might help in this period of history.

● Ask for volunteers to step, back in time, through the hoop once more. Once a child has stepped through the hoop, ask them to reveal the skills they have which will help them to survive during that historical period, for example, in Roman times and encourage them to explain why. Repeat this process of questioning for all the volunteers as they step through the hoop.

● Once all the volunteers have stepped into the past ask them what skill they think they will most need to help them survive during this period of history.

● Ask if anyone else in the class has that skill and suggest to them that travelling together might be a good idea next time.

● Have the children form teams in which the members' skills combine to be more effective than an individual's.

● Ask the children whether there are any skills that have not been mentioned which they think could be helpful in surviving in the past? You could make a list of these additional skills for future reference.

Support

● Allow children to work in pairs when completing the worksheet in order to make the task easier.

● Some children may prefer to draw pictures of themselves using the skills that they are good at or the skills that they think would 'most useful' when travelling back in time.

● Suggest to the children how the various learning and thinking skills might help when time travelling and ask the children to choose one of them to focus on. Give the children specific examples of the skills needed: an example of being 'good at using what I know' might involve choosing to tell a Roman officer about England after he has landed.

Extension

● Extend the skills range to include areas of the Multiple Intelligences: music, language, philosophy, nature, social and emotional, visual, logical and bodily.

● Choose characters from history and speculate about their own thinking and learning skills (and Multiple Intelligence profiles). Perhaps even bring these historical characters to the present day. Ask the children the following questions: *What skills might they have that would help? What skill would they need to learn quickly?*

Page

61

Time traveller

Setting the context
Meet Dr Brown. He is a time traveller. As you may know already, time travellers can travel backwards into the past or forwards into the future. However, what you may not know is that time travellers have to attend time-travelling school and become experts in either the past or the future. Dr Brown is an expert in travelling to the past but he is having difficulties at the moment. It all started when he had a rough landing and bumped his head. Ever since then his memory has been awful and he can't remember what questions to ask and what to look for to help him discover what it was like to live in the past. Next week, the top boss from the museum is joining him in his machine. Dr Brown has to show him how good he is or he may lose his expert status and even his job!

The challenge
Dr Brown has sent you a list of questions that he thinks he has used before. Can you decide which of these are good questions to ask when finding out about the past? Maybe you can add some too!

Objectives
To develop listening skills when sharing ideas.
To know that there are different ways to engage in learning.
To know some useful questions to ask when finding out about the past.

You will need
Copies of photocopiable page 67; a large sheet of card for each learner or team of learners; paper and pencils for writing additional questions; glue; safe access to pairs of scissors.

Preparation
Photocopy the questions sent by Dr Brown (see photocopiable page 67). You may want to copy enough for one each or enlarge the page so that it is big enough for groups to share. Talk with the children about how we learn. It will be useful to have completed the 'Learner Identity cards' activity from page 12, before tackling this activity. Introduce or revise 'question words' with the children and display these in the classroom.

What to do
● Read the scenario to the children and let them ask questions.
● Discuss with the children how they learn and look at their Learner ID cards if they are available. Focus on whether children like to learn alone or

Illustration © 2008, Andy Keylock / Beehive Illustration

Photograph © 2008, Scholastic Ltd

place

What are those buildings?

Where am I?

Who is in charge?

person

Can you understand me?

Where do you live?

Would you like to go for a walk?

Do you like it here?

least important

What is the time?

Where can I buy a sandwich?

check something out again.

● Tell the children they have 20 minutes to sort Dr Brown's questions and write some more of their own. They will need to present the questions on their piece of card.

Drawing together

● Display all of the children's completed cards.

● Read out each of Dr Brown's questions in turn and compare where everyone has decided to place these on their card. Listen to the children's reasons for this.

● Talk to the children about the learning experience. *Would it be good to learn alone all of the time? Is it good to always work with others? Can you think of other times when you might prefer to work with a group of children? Do you think it is helpful to listen to other children? Why?*

with a group of children. Encourage the children to decide how they want to work on this activity: alone, with a partner, in a group of three, in a large group (possibly supported by an adult). You may also want to offer a variety of different learning spaces such as a single table, a group of tables, floor space, with lights off in one area and so on.

● Introduce the questions from Dr Brown (see photocopiable page 67). Read each question aloud and talk with the children about ways of sorting them out. For example, you could have 'great' questions, 'ok' questions, 'don't use' questions, 'questions to ask first', 'questions to ask later'.

● Ask the children to tell each other what they have to do. Then invite the children to tell you what they have to do. Ask the children to indicate their level of understanding of the task, for example, by standing up if they are ready to start, putting their hands on their heads if they are not quite sure but want to begin and check again late or sitting on their hands if they want to

Support

● Provide support for reading the questions and spelling words.

● Have question words on display for less confident learners to refer to.

● The activity could be carried out as a focus activity in groups of six. This could also be facilitated by an adult who could act as a scribe for any additional questions that may be suggested.

Extension

Make a box to collect artefacts for Dr Brown. Make use of ICT by recording the questions on tape or video instead of writing them down. Role play Dr Brown time-travelling and asking questions: *what responses might he get from people in particular historical times?*

Pirate islands

Setting the context

Captain Pegleg is a famous pirate. He has sailed the seas for many years. Songs have been written about him and pirates have always queued up to be picked as one of his crew members. Captain Pegleg has remembered that you know the route around several treasure islands. He has also remembered that you agreed to give him maps of these islands by the end of the morning in exchange for two bags of gold coins. You do not have long. Captain Pegleg is a very impatient man and doesn't like to be kept waiting!

The challenge

You need to collect up all your memories about the islands. Remember to use the list that Captain Pegleg sent and don't forget to use pictures as well as labels – many of the crew can't read or write!

Objectives

To develop creative and collaboration skills within strict time limits.
To reflect on the learning process.
To explore how to make simple maps that include natural features.

You will need

A3 sheets of blue card to form the base (perhaps pre-cut in an island shape depending on the ability of the class); a variety of collage resources: tissue paper, crepe paper, art straws, shiny paper, tin foil, tinsel; paper for labels or use the pre-made labels from photocopiable page 68; a resource box/tray for each team to keep their resources together; glue; safe access to pairs of scissors. You will also need a visible way to count down 40 minutes such as a classroom clock or a sand timer. You could use a teaching clock to show the end time. Show the children how to watch the classroom clock move towards this time. You may also want a large piece of flipchart paper to record the 'Levels of success' chart during the activity. Alternatively, you could prepare this on an interactive whiteboard.

Preparation

For this activity to work, children will need to have had previous experience of writing labels. Gather the materials together and place them in plastic dishes on tables or in a central resource zone in the classroom. Make photocopies of the labels sent by Captain Pegleg (see photocopiable page 68). Prepare an outline of the 'Levels of success' chart (see below) to refer to during the activity.

Levels of success

Must	Should	Could
✔ Sea		
✔ Land		
✔ Treasure marked		

What to do

● Organise the class into small groups of three and read the scenario to them.

● Invite the children to ask questions about Captain Pegleg.

● Unfold the flipchart or show the children the whiteboard with the 'Levels of success' chart on it. Explain that Captain Pegleg has already sent a list of features that have to be on the map but that the children could impress him more by adding extra detail.

Photograph © 2008, Lynne Williams

● Ask the children to think of additional features that a map *should* have. Ask the children to think of additional features a map *could* have. Talk about the difference between 'should' and 'could'.

● Give each team three minutes of thinking time to brainstorm new ideas for the 'should' and 'could' columns of the chart.

● Ask each team to feed back their ideas and then, together, fill in the chart with some success criteria. Make sure this is on display and is easily accessible for the children during the task. Remind the children that they can refer to the chart at any time.

● Tell them they will have only 40 minutes to create their island map before it is time for Captain Pegleg to collect them.

● Explain to the children that they will be working together in threes. *What will that look like and sound like?*

Drawing together

● Ask the learners to look at their island maps and reflect on how well they have met the success criteria that were set.

● Allow each team to think of one thing they would add if they had five extra minutes. Invite each team to tell the class

about this and encourage them to ask questions about each other's maps.

● Allow the teams to add to or alter their map within the five minutes.

● Organise for someone to dress up as Captain Pegleg and arrive in class. Invite the captain to interview each team and talk about how each map should be used. Captain Pegleg should also ask questions about how the teams worked together (see 'Questions for the landlubbers' on page 68).

Support

● Provide the children with ready-made labels or limit the number of resources available to make the task easier.

● Alternatively, extend the time allowed.

Extension

More confident learners could include some buried treasure on their maps. They could also create a key for the map and a list of directions for Captain Pegleg to follow that lead to the treasure.

You're history

1. I am going back in time to _____

2. I am going to meet _____

3. The skills I have are: _____

_____

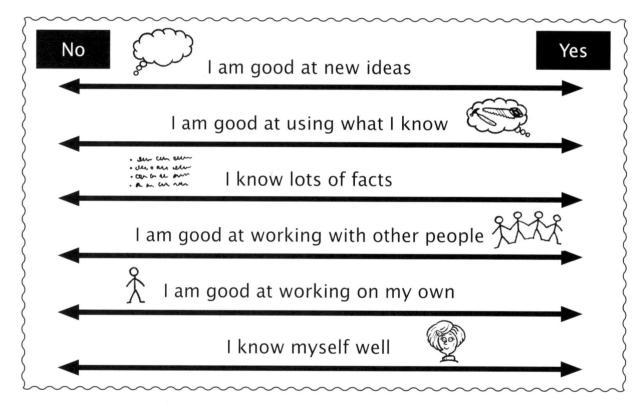

4. My most useful skill will be _____

_____

because _____

_____

5. The skill I don't have but I might need is _____

_____

because _____

_____

PHOTOCOPIABLE *Creative Activities for Thinking and Learning: Ages 5-7*

SCHOLASTIC
www.scholastic.co.uk

Time traveller

✂

Where am I?

What are those buildings?

Do you like it here?

Would you like to go for a walk?

Where can I buy a sandwich?

Who is in charge?

Where do you live?

What is the time?

Can you understand me?

Pirate islands

- Design a map for Captain Pegleg and his crew. Be ready to answer his questions or he may make you walk the plank!

Questions for the landlubbers
What be this on the map?
Why did ye choose this?
Would ye choose this again?
How did ye work together?
What happened if ye didn't all agree?
Did ye make thee walk the plank?
Can ye teach me crew to work together?
How?

- Add these labels to your map to make it easier for the crew to understand.

sea	grass	river
land	tree	rocks
treasure	cave	cliff
hill	danger	

Chapter Five

Thinking, learning and the creative arts

- Music box tales   70
- Group paintbox   72
- Under the sea   74
- Monster pizza   76
- Painting carousel   78

The five activities in this chapter all develop thinking and learning skills in the contexts of music, art and crafts.

● In **Music box tales**, the children are cast as composer/authors who must create a new idea for a movie studio. The old fairy tales are just not selling any more so fresh ideas are needed. Children work as a class to list existing fairytale characters and motifs along with a wide collection of sounds. They then combine these into a new tale and present it to the movie director for approval.

● **Group paintbox** allows children to produce a unique individual piece of artwork but then challenges them to think carefully about how their piece can be connected to the artwork of others. Cooperation in a large group can be a challenge even for adults.

Through this activity, children will become aware of how their efforts fit in with the those of others and they will also start to learn the skills of wider cooperation.

● **Under the sea** allows children to work outside to create mud sculptures. In the current educational climate, we are being encouraged to use the outdoor environment on a daily basis. Learning outside can meet the needs of a variety of children, particularly those who need to move around a lot and explore. It also opens up opportunities for environmental discussion, including issues of sustainability and responsibility; and gives greater scope for the type of activity that can be offered. Schools with no access to grass or mud can use bags of compost instead.

● In **Monster pizza**, children make pizzas out of scrap paper in an attempt to stop hungry monsters raiding the art cupboard during the night. They have to do this under strict time conditions.

● The final activity, **Painting carousel** invites children to work both independently and as part of a group to create a team painting, with each child having access to only one colour.

Music box tales

Setting the context

The Fairy Sounds Movie Studio wants new ideas for children's films. They've asked you to combine parts of stories that you know with interesting sounds to create new and exciting ideas.

The challenge

The director of the Fairy Sounds Movie Studio will be visiting you in one hour's time to look at and hear your ideas. So, get your thinking, seeing and music heads on and start creating!

Objectives

To learn how to evaluate paired work.
To learn how to arrange sounds to appropriate story themes.
To explore writing musical stories.

You will need

A selection of known fairytale texts; a selection of musical instruments; photocopiable page 80 (enough for each pair of children); lining paper and Blu-Tack® or masking tape; a marker/felt- tipped pen for each child; an animated fairytale DVD, for example, 'Hoodwinked'; copies of the 'Levels of success' chart for the children to refer to when evaluating their work at the end of the activity.

Preparation

Fix two long strips of lining paper, each at least three metres in length, to the classroom wall. Label one 'Characters' and the other 'Events and Objects'. Have to hand or at least in your mind several fairytale characters and events from fairy tales – perhaps as images in books or

ready to present to the children on an interactive whiteboard. Select and cue up a short clip of an animated fairy tale that includes a good example of where music and sounds are used to illustrate the action. Assemble a large and varied collection of musical instruments.

What to do

● Introduce the scenario and problem to the children and show them the video clip that you have chosen.

● Share a selection of fairytale characters, objects and events with the children and encourage them to offer their own ideas (for example, Snow White; a red cape; a straw house blowing down).

● Give a pen to each child and allow them five minutes to silently and independently add characters, objects and events from fairy tales to the papers on the classroom wall – they can draw or write their ideas.

● Put the children into pairs and set them the task of creating a new story by choosing two characters and three objects or events from the ideas on the wall.

● Give them five minutes to collect five ideas from the wall.

● Make sure that the pairs record their chosen ideas on the photocopiable page 80.

● Then, mix up the children, organising them into new pairs and ask them to tell each other which five ideas they have chosen from the walls.

● Share a selection of musical instruments and show how different sounds can illustrate different characters, objects or events. For example, a cymbal could represent the wind blowing; a xylophone could be the three bears; a wood block could represent the sound of an axe.

● Ask pairs of children to match a sound to each character and object or event that they have chosen.

Drawing together

● Re-form the original sets of pairs and ask

them to share their musical choices with each other.

● Ask selected pairs to demonstrate their choices to the class.

● Role play the director and give feedback on how interesting the ideas and sounds are.

● Ask pairs to assess their work using the success criteria from the chart (see below).

● Ask pairs of children to decide on one thing that they were really proud of in their task and one thing that they would like to do better next time.

Support

When organising the children into pairs, match up the more confident learners with those who are less confident. Make the task easier by providing source ideas on the walls or by limiting the choice of instruments and sounds. With another adult, model ways to improve paired work.

Extension

● Create a full story from the ideas and sounds collected. Pairs could join up into groups of four to combine their ideas. Set them a challenge to negotiate their ideas down from ten to five ideas.

● Alternatively, challenge the children to use two appropriate instruments for each of the five ideas.

Levels of success

Not there yet ☆	Nearly there ☆☆	Fantastic ☆☆☆
✔ Too many characters or objects/events chosen	✔ 1 character chosen	✔ 2 characters chosen
✔ Worked alone	✔ 2 or fewer objects/ events	✔ 3 objects/events chosen
✔ No sounds added	✔ Fewer than 5 sounds	✔ 5 different sounds to match characters or objects/events
✔ Not finished yet	✔ Most ideas recorded	
✔ No ideas recorded		✔ All ideas recorded

Group paintbox

Photograph © 2008, JupiterImages Corporation

Setting the context
The classroom badly needs some bright, colourful and interesting artwork. If everyone makes a single picture and then if all the pictures are put together, there will be enough to make a wonderful display. However, there are rules that must not be broken:
1. The picture should include green somewhere.
2. The picture should include a straight line.
3. The picture should include an animal or plant.
4. The picture should include a squiggle.
5. The picture should include a machine.

The challenge
There are five instructions for creating your artwork and you must follow three (and only three) of them.

Objectives
To learn to cooperate with others and to be able to accept not getting one's own way.
To explore and compare artwork that meets strict criteria.

You will need
A5 paper; some colouring pens or pencils; a blank, backed display board.

Preparation
Prepare the paper and make up sets of colouring pens or pencils. Prepare a sample piece of artwork which adheres to three of the five rules above.

What to do
● Explain to the children that their challenge is to create a colourful display which fulfils three criteria of their choosing from the list of five. (For

Photograph © 2008, Scholastic Ltd

example, a child who chooses 1, 4 and 5 might create a picture of a machine that makes long, green, stringy, sweets. In this picture there would not be any straight lines, animals or plants (2 and 3). The choice of 1, 2 and 4 could produce a more abstract piece, but without any animals, plants or machines (3 and 5).

● Tell the children that they can add other things not in the rules but their three choices must be featured in the picture and the remaining two must not be included.

● Illustrate how you followed the rules by showing the children your sample that you prepared earlier, and discuss it with them.

● Set the children to work.

Drawing together

● As the children finish their artwork, bring them back together as a whole class.

● Select several pieces of finished work and ask the artists to show where their three chosen rules feature.

● Show some of the other pieces and challenge the children to identify the three chosen rules.

● Then introduce the rules for assembling the class display: each piece of artwork must be next to at least one other piece; each piece must share two or more rules with those next to it.

● Ask the children to find a partner whose work will fit with theirs by sharing these two rules.

● Then, ask pairs to get together and fit their four pieces together according to the rules.

● Where good matches occur, use Blu-Tack® to stick the work to the display board. (Be aware that the rules may create an interesting arrangement of pieces.)

● Continue until all the pieces are displayed.

Photograph © 2008, Scholastic Ltd

For those pieces which cannot be joined together because of the rules, begin another piece of artwork on a different part of the board.

Support

You can make the task much simpler by choosing only one rule to include or by reducing the number and variety of rules. Make mini-displays of only four to eight pieces to make the 'putting together' more straightforward.

Extension

● Increase the number of rules and the number of choices.

● Give pairs of children all the pieces of finished artwork and challenge them to create a new display.

● Create large-scale displays by working with other classes, the whole year group or the whole school.

● Look at the display of another group or class and challenge your class to work out their rules.

Under the sea

Setting the context
Ollie the Octopus and Rainbow Fish are very lonely. They used to live in a part of the ocean where they had lots of friends, but one day they decided to pack up and go on an adventure. They found a nice spot to set up camp and, after a while, they decided to live there. Now, they sit each evening in their underground cave watching videos and looking at photos of their old friends. Suddenly, Ollie the Octopus has a fantastic idea – they could make models of their old friends until they meet some new sea creatures to be friends with. They are surrounded by mud, they are good with their fins and they can remember exactly what their friends look like. They could make mud sculptures of their old friends!

The challenge
Are you ready to become mud sculptors and help Ollie the Octopus and Rainbow Fish to make sculptures of their friends?

Objectives
To develop creative thinking and collaboration skills within strict time limits.
To learn to handle lots of ideas and make choices.
To be able to evaluate a final product by creating a list of success criteria and assessing the product against this.
To make a simple 3D shape using natural materials.

You will need
Mud; water, a small bucket and two small spades or equivalent for each team; a variety of leaves, twigs and stones; pencils; photocopiable pages 81 and 82; a large plastic sheet or equivalent on which the children can make their mud sculptures. You will also need a visible way to count down 20 minutes such as, a sand timer or an electronic timer.

Preparation
Before you introduce the activity, spend some time looking at a variety of pictures of sea creatures with the children. Use books, posters, photographs, or create a Powerpoint® presentation. Discuss the features and shapes of the sea creatures. Photocopy page 81 for each team. Photocopy and cut up the sea-life cards (see page 82).

What to do
● Organise the children into groups of three. Explain the scenario to them and let them ask questions.
● Talk about the pictures of sea

Illustration © 2008, Andy Keylock / Beehive Illustration

Photographs © 2008, Lynne Williams

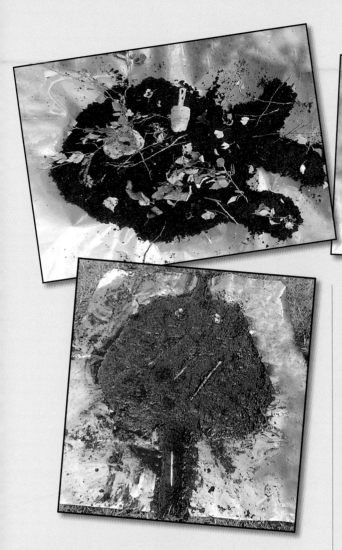

Drawing together

● Ask the learners to look at their mud sculpture and reflect on how well they have met the criteria that they wrote on their checklist.

● Ask each team what they thought they did well and what they would do differently next time.

● Organise a mud sculpture gallery outside. Allow time for the teams to wander around, looking at all the different creations. Encourage parents and other classes to do the same.

● Ensure that all of the children wash their hands thoroughly after this activity!

creatures and remind the children of their discussions about such creatures in previous lessons.

● Give out one sea-life card to each team or allow them to pick one from a 'face-down' pile.

● Make sure each team understands the word on their card.

● Introduce 'thinking and planning' time. Discuss how everyone has ideas and that they are all important. Tell each team to fill the light bulb on their worksheet with ideas about what features to include for their sea creature. Allow five minutes for this task.

● Now, tell each team to sort through their ideas and choose five ideas to write at the bottom of the sheet. These ideas will be used as a criteria checklist to assess their mud sculpture at the end of the activity.

● Tell the children that they will only have 20 minutes to create their mud sculpture.

● Tell them that they will be working together – *what will that look like and sound like?* Then set the teams to work.

Support

● Organise groups carefully so that children are able to support each other.

● Role play what it looks like to come up with lots of ideas and make choices – this could be achieved through a circle time session.

● Limit the number of resources or extend the time allowed and provide an example of a criteria checklist to make the activity easier.

Extension

Challenge the children to write a description of their mud sculpture experience. They could also write down their solutions for making choices about which ideas to use.

Monster pizza

Setting the context

It's a well-known fact that monsters like to eat lots of food. It's also a well-known fact that monsters are not seen very much. What is not so well known is that monsters are a big problem to school caretakers. School caretakers won't admit to this! I mean, who would believe them? Monsters only come to school at night – that's when they are feeling hungry. But they don't stop at the kitchen. They don't touch the leftover packed lunches and they even ignore the teachers' cupboard where the secret chocolate bars are kept! What these monsters like to eat most is the resources from the art cupboard and every time they do this, they make a big mess for the caretaker to clean up! The caretaker has had an idea! He wants to leave monster pizzas outside the cupboard to stop the monsters feeling hungry, opening the art cupboard and making a mess.

The challenge

Can you help the caretaker create a set of monster pizzas? You'll have to hurry, the pizzas must be ready by the end of the afternoon.

Objectives

To develop decision-making skills when working to time limits.
To develop an understanding of planning, designing, modelling, modifying and reflecting.
To learn to handle lots of ideas and make choices.

You will need

A variety of 'scrap' art resources (from the cupboard); glue; pieces of card to act as pizza bases; pencils; colouring pencils or felt-tipped pens; photocopiable page 83; a prepared note from the caretaker saying which one of the art resources he has realised the monsters do not like. You will also need a visible way to count down 20 minutes such as a sand timer or an electronic timer.

Preparation

Look at a variety of pictures of pizzas with the children. These could be taken from books, posters, photographs or a Powerpoint® presentation. For a real introduction to pizzas, invite a local chef or the school cook into school to talk to the children. You may find it useful to read stories that contain pizzas in the lead up to this activity. Children will be able to visualise a 'whole' pizza if they have seen pictures or photographs beforehand – many children may only have seen a 'slice of pizza' when they have eaten it for their dinner. You may also want to discuss the layers that make up a pizza and how the ingredients are placed

NOTES

The monster does
not like to eat:

the colour blue

Signed,
The caretaker.

Illustration © 2008, Andy Keylock / Beehive Illustration

onto the plate. Photocopy enough worksheets from page 83 for each team. Collect together a range of 'scrap' art resources.

What to do

● Organise the children into groups of three. Explain the scenario to them and let them ask questions.

● Talk about the pictures of pizzas and remind the children of their previous discussions and activities. Tell them that the caretaker has come to them for help because they are experts in pizzas.

● Introduce 'thinking and planning' time. Discuss how everyone has ideas and that they are all important. Let the children see the scrap resources that are available. Ask questions to focus the planning such as: *What makes a pizza a pizza? What does a pizza look like?*

● Tell each team to talk about their ideas and design what their own pizza will look like by filling the pizza base on their worksheet with their design ideas. Allow ten minutes for this task.

● Tell the children that they will have only 20 minutes to create their monster pizza using the 'scrap' art materials.

● Explain that they will be working together – *what will that look like and sound like?*

● Interrupt the process and tell the children that you have just had a message from the caretaker. Read out the caretaker's note – this will describe one type of art material that the monsters do not like. Ask the children why this shouldn't be included on their pizza. They will then need to reassess and modify their pizzas.

Drawing together

● At the end of the activity, ask the children to take their pizzas to the art cupboard and leave them outside. Return in the morning to see if the pizzas have been eaten.

● Evaluate with the children whether making the pizzas solved the problem of the hungry monsters making a mess.

Photograph © 2008, JupiterImages Corporation

Page
77

Support

● Limit the amount of resources available or extend the time allowed.

● Organise groups so that children are able to support each other.

● Use 'freeze' moments throughout the activity to draw the class back together, give feedback and readdress issues.

Extension

● Introduce fractions by telling the children how many monsters are coming and challenge them to cut the pizza equally into this many pieces.

● Look at recipes for pizzas and make pizzas as part of a follow-up activity. The children could then write their own recipes for a monster pizza.

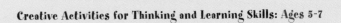

Painting carousel

Setting the context
I was having a big clear out of my attic at the weekend and I found something really interesting. It was stuck in the corner of an old box. It looks like it could be a letter. Shall we open it? (Read the letter from photocopiable page 84.) I don't think that Matilda ever opened this letter. That's really sad because now we'll never know whether Paul's idea ever worked, unless… would you all like to try it out?

The challenge
Can you make Paul's idea work?

Objectives
To develop independent working and collaboration skills within a group task.
To improve observation skills.
To learn to take a risk and to persevere.

You will need
A copy of the letter from photocopiable page 84; small paper plates with one paint colour for each team member; paintbrushes; aprons; pieces of paper; For each team, you will also need a copy of the famous painting they are reproducing. Postcards of paintings can be bought from galleries or art shops.

Preparation
Look at a variety of Paul Klee's paintings – or whichever artist you choose to use. You may find it useful to have introduced paintings from a variety of artists and discussed colour, line and shape in each of these. You may also like to encourage the children to reproduce their own interpretations of these paintings before starting this activity. Arrange pieces of paper and the plates with paint around a table, so that each child in a team has a different colour.

Plate © 2008 JupiterImages Corporation. Paint © Scholastic Ltd

Illustration © 2008 Andy Keylock / Beehive Illustration

Illustration © 2008, Scholastic Ltd

the paint colours that are available. Ask questions to focus the planning: *Who will use which colour paint? How will you know when to move onto the next piece of paper? What happens if someone paints their colour where you think yours should have gone – does this matter? How can you help each other? What if one of you gets stuck or upset?*

● Tell the children that they will be working on their own on a piece of paper but that the group needs to help each other as well. *What will that look like and sound like?*

Drawing together

● Bring together the paintings from each group. Use the following questions to begin the discussions and evaluations: *Are they all the same? Why not? Does it matter that they are the same/not the same? What did you find hard about this activity? Did you like this activity? Why? Do you think it helped you to work together? Did you feel worried about not getting it right for your team? Why did or didn't you give up? What would you do differently next time?*

What to do

● Create groups of five children. Read Matilda's letter to the children and allow them to ask questions.
● Search with the children for some of the paintings, possibly using the internet.
● Discuss as a class which would be the best painting to try to work on together.
● Talk about the process of walking around the table – a bit like a fairground ride going around and around. You may want to practise or demonstrate doing this at one table. Each child starts on one piece of paper and looks at the famous painting – they paint only where they see their colour. They then move onto the next piece of paper and add their colour. Repeat the process until all the pieces of paper are finished.
● Introduce 'Thinking and planning' time. Discuss how everyone has opinions and that they are all important. Let the children see

Support

● Organise the groups carefully so that children are able to support each other.
● Use 'freeze' moments during the activity to draw the class back together, give feedback and readdress issues.
● Model different parts of the activity first, with you (as the teacher) joining the group and being the one to get it wrong – discuss this.

Extension

● Add white and/or black to each plate as well as the initial colour.
● Ask each group to decide on one extra colour to use that is not in the famous painting – how will they use this?

Music box tales

- Choose two characters for your story.
- Choose three objects or events for your story.
- Create a sound for each character, object or event.
- Write or draw your ideas below.

Character	Character	Object/Event	Object/Event	Object/Event
Sound	Sound	Sound	Sound	Sound

■ SCHOLASTIC
www.scholastic.co.uk

Under the sea (1)

- Listen to everyone in your team and write a list of ideas for your sea creature on the light bulb.

- Now choose five ideas from your list that you will include on your mud sculpture and write them in the boxes.

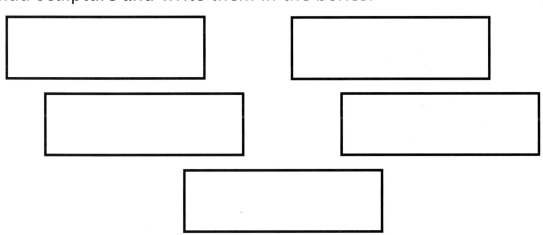

Illustration © 2008, Gemma Hastilow

PHOTOCOPIABLE **Creative Activities for Thinking and Learning Skills: Ages 5-7**

Under the sea (2)

starfish	dolphin
octopus	sea horse
fish	stingray
shark	whale
crab	jellyfish

SCHOLASTIC
www.scholastic.co.uk

Monster pizzas

- Make a plan for your monster pizza.

- You may want to add some labels and numbers. (The numbers might show the order in which the items should be added.)

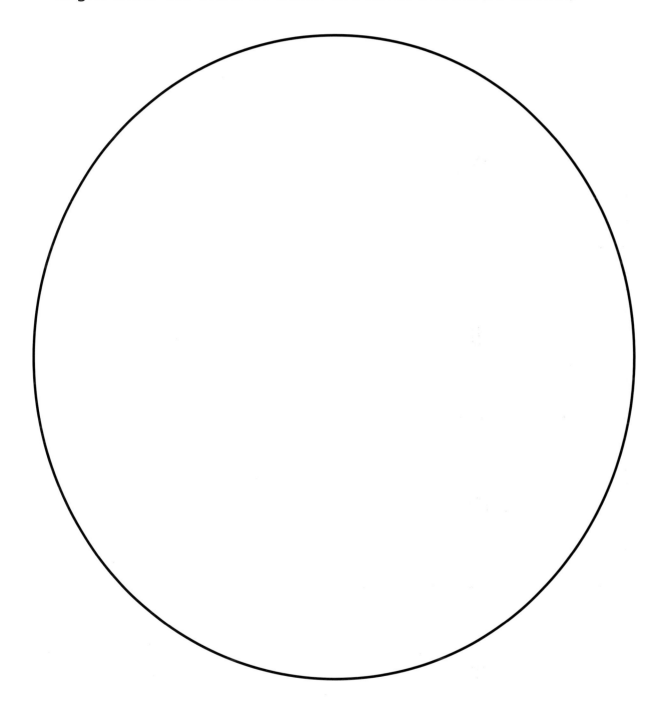

■SCHOLASTIC
www.scholastic.co.uk
PHOTOCOPIABLE *Creative Activities for Thinking and Learning Skills: Ages 5-7*

Painting carousel

My dearest Matilda,

I've been working on a painting lately and I have some students coming in to look at it. They are going to be paying a lot of money for me to teach them but they don't talk to each other or get on. This makes it really hard.

Anyway, they all want to have a go at reproducing my painting. I have had a clever plan that might get them talking to each other! I'm going to give them one colour each. They are in charge of that colour: no one else can use it. So they must work together and help complete each other's painting! They will need to talk to each other first.

Do you think this will work? I really value your advice.

My best wishes to you,

Paul Klee

Chapter Six

Thinking, learning and PE

- All-team rounders   86
- The jungle dance   88
- Alien walk   90
- On safari   92

The following four activities teach thinking and learning skills through PE.

● In **All-team rounders**, children play and develop a new version of rounders that reduces the amount of time spent standing around. From a child's point of view, team games such as rounders often involve very long periods of waiting, punctuated by very short periods of excitement: children queue to bat or linger on the field waiting to catch the ball, then they are suddenly facing the bowler and getting ready to hit and run. All-team rounders is an excellent way to keep all team members involved throughout the game.

● **The jungle dance** requires children to invent a dance for a particular jungle animal to perform in a parade. They need to work in a team and explore ways to make the dance memorable as they only have 15 minutes to learn it! If you spend time beforehand researching with the children the variety of animals that live in a jungle, their ideas are likely to be more informed and more imaginative.

● In **Alien walk**, the children receive a letter from their alien friend, Odit, inviting them to visit his planet in outer space. In order to go there, however, they must learn how to walk like an alien. The activity requires children to work in groups and invent an alien walk. The walk must follow strict alien rules and should be easy enough for everyone in the group to remember and learn in a short space of time.

● **On safari** asks the children to imagine being intrepid adventurers. They are about to meet their biggest challenge yet! The activity tests the children's ability to collaborate with each other, think strategically and evaluate their thinking and actions as they plan an appropriate route around an obstacle course.

All-team rounders

Setting the context
The Supreme World Council of Children has issued an order to reduce the amount of time that the children of the world have to stand around waiting for things. Your school has decided to adopt a new version of rounders to show how easy these changes can be made but not all the rules have been decided yet.

The challenge
Can you think of any rules to improve all-team rounders?

Objectives
To work collaboratively in a team.
To develop strategic and tactical thinking.
To improve skills in running, hitting a ball and passing a ball.

You will need
Five small, soft cones; one rounders bat; one ball.

Preparation
Set up a standard rounders pitch and organise the children into two well-matched teams.

What to do
● Explain the following rules to the children:

1. All-team rounders is similar to normal rounders but there is very little waiting around.

2. The batter gets three chances to hit the ball.

3. When he/she chooses to run, all the other batters must follow him/her in a safe line. Their aim is to all get back to the start.

4. When all the batters have made it back, the last batter raises his/her hand and shouts 'Batters in'.

5. While the batters are running, all the fielders must run to where the ball has landed.

6. All the fielders must then line up, make a tunnel with the legs and pass (or roll) the ball through all their legs, from one end of the tunnel to the other.

7. When the last fielder receives the ball, he/she holds it in the air and shouts 'Fielders through'.

8. The team that calls first gets one point.

9. The bowler must be changed for each new batter.

10. This continues until everyone has had a chance to bat and bowl, with teams

swapping roles half way through.

11. Warn the children to take care where they run. Depending on where the ball goes, batters and fielders can get very tangled. Do not yet give a rule for what to do in this circumstance.

● The game is pretty straightforward but will provide the opportunity for many strategies and tactics to emerge.

● Eventually the two lines will get in each other's way. When this happens, stop the game and ask the children to suggest a rule. For example, batters must run around the fielders' line. Other potential problems with the game are that batters will try to send the ball to places where it is difficult for fielders to line up, or fielders may hover in the place where they expect the ball to land.

● Allow the game to develop, with tactics and rules being added from the children's suggestions, bearing safety in mind.

Drawing together

● Bring the children back together.

● Ask them to discuss with a partner how they played the game and the clever tricks that they invented to help their team.

● Ask them if further rules are needed.

● Ask them to compare all-team rounders to normal rounders. *Which is best and why?*

Support

● Simplify the game by playing it in smaller teams of between four and eight children.

● Some children may prefer to use a wide bat or a larger ball. Impose additional rules from the start to avoid players crashing into each other.

Extension

● Change the activity that each team has to perform, for example, batters have to run to a fixed point and back; fielders have to each touch the ball twice.

● Impose time limits for the game to make the teams work harder. Change the size of the bat, the ball or the pitch to vary the game.

Illustration © 2008, Andy Keylock / Beehive Illustration

The jungle dance

Photograph © 2008, JupiterImages Corporation

Setting the context

Strange things are beginning to happen in the classroom. You start to hear some drums in the distance and the floor seems to shake a little. As you all stare at each other in wonder, you realise that trees are growing around you and it is getting hotter. You blink and rub your eyes. As your vision becomes clear again you all look around in amazement. Here you are in the middle of a jungle! You can hear jungle noises, birds calling to each other, the movement of trees, the sound of a waterfall nearby and the cry of jungle animals. Then you look at yourselves. You are no longer boys and girls. You have turned into jungle animals. Then you hear a loud voice echo through the jungle: 'Calling all jungle animals! Gather in 15 minutes! The jungle parade is about to begin'.

The challenge

The jungle parade starts in 15 minutes. Which animal are you going to be? How should you move and sound?

Objectives

To improve collaboration skills within a set time limit.
To remember, sort and sequence ideas.
To explore linking basic actions in a sequence using different shapes, levels and directions of travel.

You will need

A set of animal cards from photocopiable page 94; jungle type music (optional); access to the hall or a large area suitable for PE; a timer or a clock; a parade route laid out – possibly using chalk or ropes laid on the floor.

Preparation

You may find it useful to have researched jungle animals with the class before introducing this activity. Photocopy the animal cards from page 94 and cut them out. Source a CD player and some jungle music (optional). List the dance checklist on large piece of flipchart paper to refer to with the children and prepare a blank 'Levels of success' chart on a whiteboard or a flipchart to complete with the children during the activity.

What to do

● Organise the children into groups of four. Read the scenario to the children and let them ask questions about the task.
● Discuss what they already know about jungle animals – you may want to direct their thoughts to the specific jungle animals in your focus activity.
● Give out the animal cards – let each group choose a card or ask one child from each group to pick one from a 'face-down' pile.
● Point out the checklist for the animal dance:
　　1. Your dance must suit the animal you have chosen.
　　2. You must choose three different movements for the animal.
　　3. You must choose two different sounds for your animal.

4. You must put them into a sequence that you repeat over and over again.

5. You must make sure that everyone in your team remembers the movements.

6. Your animal dance must be ready for the parade in 15 minutes.

● Give the children an opportunity to clarify their understanding with you.

● Ask the children to think about what a successful jungle dance would look like and complete the 'Levels of success' chart with them.

● Tell the children that they will have only 15 minutes to remember, sort and sequence their ideas. Discuss what this means.

Drawing together

● When the 15 minutes is up, announce that all animals have to join the parade and sit either side of the jungle track that you have created.

● Ask for a volunteer team to go first and show their animal dance to the class. They repeat it over and over until they reach the end of the track.

● Ask teams to identify which animal was being depicted. Repeat until all teams have exhibited their animal dance.

● Ask teams to look at the success criteria they created and discuss how well they did with the animal dance. They should consider what they would do differently next time, what they found easy about the task and what they found hard.

Support

● Simplify the task through careful organisation of groups and by negotiating additional time if teams are not ready. Structure the session and use 'freeze' moments during the task to draw the class back together, give feedback and readdress issues.

● Model different parts of the activity first, with you, the teacher, joining a group and being the one to get it wrong. Discuss how to react and deal with this.

Extension

● Ask each team to follow the performing team along the parade track and copy the repeated movements.

● Ask each team to make a list of the movements and sounds in their dance. Pair up two teams and ask the teams to teach each other and assess each other's dance.

Example of a 'Levels of success' chart using children's ideas

Not there yet ☆	Nearly there ☆☆	Fantastic ☆☆☆
✔ 1 movement ✔ 1 sound ✔ Not repeated	✔ 3 movements ✔ 1 sound ✔ Almost everyone remembers	✔ 3 movements ✔ 2 sounds ✔ Repeated over and over and easy to copy ✔ Everyone remembers

Alien walk

Setting the context

You have received a letter from your alien friend, Odit, inviting you to visit his planet. How exciting! However, there is work to do and you need the help of your friends. In order to visit Odit's planet you need to be able to do the alien walk.

Aliens walk everywhere in a particular way and they wouldn't like it if you couldn't do the same.

The challenge

Can you learn to do an alien walk?

Objectives

To develop collaboration skills within a set time limit.

To recognise the role of a leader as someone who helps everyone else to achieve a common goal.

To develop organisational skills to navigate an obstacle course.

To improve control and use of different shapes, levels and direction of travel.

You will need

A flipchart or whiteboard; access to the hall or a large area suitable for PE; a timer or a clock; an obstacle course already set out; small whiteboards; scrap paper; pencils.

Preparation

Prepare the following alien-walk rules on a whiteboard or flipchart:

1. Aliens do not walk forwards.
2. Aliens never walk alone.
3. Aliens can only sidestep, hop, jump and twist.
4. Aliens never run.
5. Aliens do one special thing when they walk.

Prepare an obstacle course which the children will see before planning their alien walk. Alternatively, set up individual obstacle courses for each team depending on how large your hall space is.

What to do

● Create groups of five children. Read the scenario to them and invite them to ask questions about the task.

● Point out the alien rules for the alien walk (see Preparation). Give the children the opportunity to clarify their understanding with you.

● Create a 'Levels of success' chart to explore what a successful alien walk would look like (see example below). Put all the alien-walk rules into the 'Fantastic' column and ask learners to think about what it would look like if their alien walk was: 'Nearly there' or 'Not there yet'. Record their ideas in the chart.

● Tell them that they will have only 15 minutes to remember, sort and sequence their ideas. Discuss what this means.

● Remind the children that it is very important to the success of the task to ensure that everyone in their group remembers the movements of the alien walk.

Drawing together

● Ask all the teams to sit around the edge of the obstacle course.

● Then, using the flipchart, point out the rules of an alien walk to remind the children of what should have been incorporated.

● Observe each team complete the obstacle course using their alien walk.

● Encourage each team to self-assess their performance, saying what they liked and what they would do better. Invite the children who are sitting and observing to identify what they thought the 'performing' team did well according to the success criteria.

● Ask all of the teams to consider the following questions: *What would you do differently next time? What did you find easy about the task? What did you find hard? How did you organise yourselves? How did having a leader of your team help?*

Support

● If children are struggling to come up with an alien walk, allow additional time.

● Use 'freeze' moments to draw the class back together, give feedback and readdress issues.

Extension

● Pair up two teams and ask the teams to teach each other their alien walks and then to assess each other's walk.

● Invite the children to write a letter to Odit explaining how they have practised the alien walk.

Levels of success

Not there yet ☆	Nearly there ☆ ☆	Fantastic ☆ ☆ ☆
		✔ No walking forward
		✔ Always walk together
		✔ Sidestep
		✔ Hop
		✔ Jump
		✔ Twist
		✔ No running seen
		✔ One special thing

On safari

Setting the context

You are a team of experienced explorers. You have been on many adventures together and faced many dangers. However this is your biggest adventure so far. You have been asked to trek across an unknown land to rescue some precious treasure. You will need to use all of your experience of movement to make sure that everyone in your team arrives safely. There are many dangers along the way so you will need to decide carefully as a team how to avoid any disasters. Make sure you consider all your expert moves and decide which ones are the best to use to successfully complete the safari trail.

The challenge

Can your team agree on how to move through each section of the journey carefully, safely and in the best possible way?

Objectives

To develop collaboration and cooperation skills in order to reach a consensus.
To evaluate options and make decisions.
To explore linking basic actions in sequence.

You will need

A set of cards for each team from photocopiable page 95; Post-it Notes®; access to the hall or a large area suitable for PE; a timer or a clock; a piece of A3 paper; some Blu-Tack® or equivalent. You will also need various pieces of PE apparatus: mats (water), benches (bridges), spot markers (swamps), cones (trees), tables and planks (rocks).

Preparation

Photocopy the cards from page 95, cut them out and laminate them if possible. You will need one complete set of 15 cards for each team (five are movement cards, five show how to move and five are safari areas). On the Post-it Notes®, draw a smiley face on

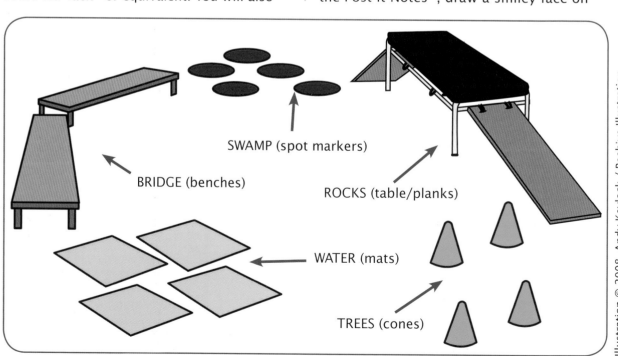

SWAMP (spot markers)

BRIDGE (benches)

ROCKS (table/planks)

WATER (mats)

TREES (cones)

Illustration © 2008, Andy Keylock / Beehive Illustration.

one and a 'wish stick' on the other. You should have two Post-it Notes® per team. Write the movement checklist (see below) on a whiteboard or flipchart for discussion during the activity. Set out the apparatus in a circuit to make a safari trail. It may be helpful to the children if you label each area with words or pictures to depict which part of the safari trail it represents.

What to do

● Create groups of three to five children.
● Introduce the safari trail to them. Talk about each area. You may want to add dangers by saying things like: *Watch out for the crocodiles in the swamp* and so on.
● Give out the cards a set at a time. Read the words together and discuss why there are three sets.
● Point out the success criteria for moving through the safari trail, using the checklist:

1. For each of the safari areas, you must choose one movement card and one card that describes how to move.
2. Your team must agree on these choices together.
3. You must prepare a plan that shows these choices.
4. Your team leader must be prepared to explain this plan to the class.
5. You must organise which order you are going in.
6. Every member must complete the movements as stated on your plan.

● Give the children an opportunity to clarify their understanding with you
● Tell them they will have only 10 minutes to make their decisions and prepare their plan.
● Discuss how the teams will listen to everyone's ideas with questions such as *Can you take it in turns? How would it be best to sit if you are discussing ideas – in a line, in a circle? Can you think of a quick way to show that you agree?*

Drawing together

● When the 10 minutes are up, announce that all the safari teams have to sit either side of the safari trail that you have created. Ask for a volunteer team to go first. The team leader must first explain their plan to the class. Repeat until all the teams have completed the safari trail.
● Ask the teams to gather together and decide as a team which part of the safari trail they did really well, then instruct them to place the smiley face there.
● Then they should decide which part they wish they could have done better on and ask them to place the wish stick Post-it Note® there. Discuss what they could do to improve on this next time.

Support
● Allow additional time if teams are not ready.
● Model different parts of the activity first, with you, the teacher, joining the group and being the one to get it wrong. Discuss the children's reactions to this. Alternatively, you could make the decisions as a class initially and all follow the same movements, then move into group work later.
● Use less apparatus to simplify the task.

Extension
● Pair up two teams and ask them to teach each other and assess each other's movements. Make up a success criteria chart that depicts levels of success for each movement and assess the teams according to this.
● Challenge the children further by adding additional apparatus.

Jungle dance

gorilla 	elephant 
crocodile 	lion 
giraffe 	snake 
parrot 	zebra 

■SCHOLASTIC
www.scholastic.co.uk

On safari

slide	jump	sidestep
roll	hop	high
backwards	slowly	forwards
fast	trees	swamp
bridge	water	rocks

SCHOLASTIC

In this series:

ISBN 978-1407-10005-0

ISBN 978-1407-10006-7

Also available:

Shortlisted for the
EDUCATIONAL RESOURCES AWARDS 2005

ISBN 978-0439-94500-4

ISBN 978-0439-94501-1

ISBN 978-0439-97111-9

ISBN 978-0439-97112-6

ISBN 978-0439-97113-3

ISBN 978-0439-96526-2

ISBN 978-0439-96525-5

ISBN 978-0439-96524-8

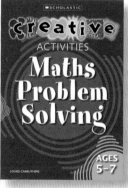

ISBN 978-0439-96556-9

ISBN 978-0439-96570-5

Available for Scotland:

ISBN 978-1407-10088-3

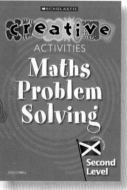

ISBN 978-1407-10089-0

ISBN 978-1407-10060-9

ISBN 978-1407-10061-6

To find out more, call: 0845 603 9091 or visit our website www.scholastic.co.uk